# THE ART OF SOULMAKING

## A PATH TO UNCONDITIONAL FREEDOM

Nicole Daedone

with Beth Wareham

soulmaker | PRESS

**soulmaker | PRESS**

soulmakerpress.com

ISBN: 978-1-961064-01-0

# CONTENTS

## Part II: Building Your House of Soul    137

## Epilogue    229

# PREFACE

I encountered *The Art of Soulmaking* after more than twenty-five years' experience in the publishing industry. I was at the top of my career, and had an adventurous lifestyle to complement the productivity. I'd edited and was a publicist for several best-selling books, and got to see parts of the world few ever get to travel to.

Then, life came crumbling down after I lost half of my family in a six-week period. It was a reckoning unlike anything I'd experienced, and I was forced to take a step back and process the trauma. With much pain, I began my journey inward, taking steps in a long process of rebuilding my internal world.

It was during this phase of my life that I was contacted by a woman who worked for Soulmaker Press, asking whether I'd be interested in editing a book called *The Art of Soulmaking*. She said the book was meant to offer a template for getting in touch with the soul, and was being written for people in prison.

One thing led to another, I met Nicole, and we started to talk about this book. At first, I had no idea what she was talking about. My idea of "practice" was squats and lunges, or things kids did on weekday evenings before their weekend soccer match. "Soul" was foreign to me as a word used outside of a religious context. I was intrigued. I had long ago abandoned religion because I didn't like the way it felt for me: binding and full of superstition and control. It didn't seem very welcoming for this much woman. No, religion was not for me. But soul, that word had energy; that word had freedom. That word had space. I said Yes, let's write the book.

I told myself my soul was no different from any other part of me—say a glute or a quad muscle—and the more I worked it, the better I'd feel. Turned out, it was as simple as that. Daily practice got me journaling and meditating and stretching. That first forty minutes of the day became sacred. Journaling was a boon to my creativity and to understanding my emotions. The more I practiced, the more insights and epiphanies I had, seemingly without effort. They just appeared, and my life deepened. I began a new relationship with the natural world, watching birds and just feeling the surging energy of Earth under my feet.

In a matter of months, as my own life changed, we finished the prison edition of the book. It launched at a women's prison in California, where, after putting up flyers, seventy-three women signed up. The prison was as shocked as we were. That was just under three years ago. Today, over 20,000 people in prison have gone through *The Art of Soulmaking: Prison Edition* book. There are dozens of formal and informal groups at over 190 prisons across the country studying the book together. Volunteer pen pals and the incarcerated participants in The Art of Soulmaking exchange tens of thousands of letters annually.

It was during this time that Nicole contacted me and suggested we make a version of this book available for the everyday person. I immediately said Yes. Again, we got to work.

It is from this personal journey, this unique and timely friendship with Nicole, and this wonderful community of people in prison, that I offer you this template to truly find yourself, and *soulmake* with your life.

You'll find plenty of instruction, encouragement, stories, and support inside this book. Embrace it as best you can, in whatever way fits for you. There's no wrong way to do it. We welcome you to this community and to this experience of freedom thousands have already benefited from.

Love,
Beth

# LETTERS TO THE NEWCOMER

In the following pages you will find two letters from individuals who've studied and followed *The Art of Soulmaking* (AoS) program. One is written by a man who served thirty-three years on death row before being executed in the spring of 2023. The other, by a woman who is a retired pastor. Both were eager to provide advice for the newcomer who encounters this path. Two additional letters are included in the back of this book.

*Letter to The Art of Soulmaking Newcomer:*

*We all want to be free. Whether we dwell in a prison cell block or live in a luxurious home, there is a longing for the freedom from our innermost fears. Freedom from the internal voice that says "I'm unworthy" and fills us with unhealthy guilt and shame. It's also the source of our self-destructive patterns, whether they be self-doubts or the feeling of hopelessness. The prisons we build inside us are way more restrictive than any prison made of concrete, bars, and barbed wire could ever be. I know this because like you, I, too have dwelled in both.*

*This program offers us a way of breaking out of our inner prisons and finding self-liberation. Many of the ideas may seem a little bizarre, but if you take the time to study and put what's written into practice, you might be surprised with the outcome. What is there to lose for giving it a go?*

*Some of the things you will learn are self-compassion, and how to view your past in a better light. You will learn how to embrace all aspects of your personal makeup which will give you more strength and a sense of completeness.*

*This is not a program that's going to judge you, nor is it going to tell you what you should or are supposed to do. Instead, it offers simple yet effective ways for you to discover the inner freedom that's possible regardless of what your circumstance or situation might be. It doesn't matter who you are or what you may have done, unconditional freedom is yours for the having. So, are you willing to take this opportunity and discover new possibilities you never thought possible before? Inner freedom is yours.*

*BRIGHTEST BLESSINGS*
*Donald Dillbeck*

Donald was incarcerated at the age of fifteen, and was executed in 2023, after thirty-three years imprisoned in the State of Florida. Donald was an active participant, mentor, and advocate for The Art of Soulmaking program.

*To the Newcomers, Welcome!*

*I'm writing as someone who has found participating in The Art of Soulmaking to be life-giving and transformative. I hope you will, too.*

*I began about a year ago as a volunteer pen pal writing to prisoners. I'm an old woman (in my late seventies) and a retired pastor who just moved to a new state. I've been on a spiritual path most of my life, and have appreciated many traditions, as well as those who seek to know themselves and find their own truths. I love AoS's basic principles, especially that we engage as equals.*

*I learn so much from my pen pals. Often, I have found I am confronted with a different interpretation of ideas I've held for a long time. The chance to reappraise, and to enlarge my perspective, or to revisit personal issues, is sometimes uncomfortable but always valuable.*

*It is a privilege to share another's journey, and I find inspiration in doing so.*

*The program invites us to learn more about ourselves, and it gives us useful tools. Some come naturally to me, some not—I have to do yoga daily because my aging body hurts if I don't, but meditation I confess to doing irregularly. However, every time I return to sit, I'm glad I did. Not because I'm "good at it," but because it settles me down.*

*I usually find Soul Letters to be very powerful. As I sit down to write I am reminded of a very old spiritual tradition of going on a pilgrimage to some sacred place. These pilgrims often walked for many weeks; most were poor and slept in the rough. (Don't think high-tech hiking gear or a comfy car and nice motels.) Most people set out seeking a miracle—such as healing, relief from pain, forgiveness, or a reunion with a lost loved one. But the 'miracles' granted were often the personal growth and understanding gained along the way, rather than the changes originally hoped for. This is what we all really gain in our journeys with The Art of Soulmaking: understanding how we can flourish in our current circumstances however difficult they may be.*

*May each of you find blessings of Companionship and Peace on your journey.*

*Anne*

A retired Episcopal priest and psychotherapist, Anne is a volunteer letter writer with The Art of Soulmaking program.

# HOW TO TAKE THIS COURSE

We'd like to impart a few suggestions on how to approach soulmaking through this book.

*The Art of Soulmaking* is broken down into twenty-six lessons. Each lesson delves into one soulmaking principle followed by integration questions.

The lessons build on one another, so while you can flip around leisurely, it's suggested that on your first read you move from one lesson to the next, in sequential order.

Time is not important here. We've seen people practice one lesson per week, completing all the lessons in six months. We've seen people go through this entire book in a week. We've seen people pick this book up, put it down, and pick it back up fifty times over the course of two years. Any way you go about it, you may experience important changes in your life. The path you choose through the book is really up to you.

We introduce instruction in yoga, meditation, and Soul Inventory at the beginning of the book so you can build a foundation of contemplative practice right away. We suggest that if you start with these practices, you start small. Very small. Ten minutes of yoga, maybe five minutes of meditation. You can build from there. What we offer here will get you started. You may choose to explore instruction elsewhere to go deeper or stay with the basics we've laid out.

You can study this book alone, in a group, with a friend, or even enroll in The Art of Soulmaking volunteer program, through the nonprofit Unconditional Freedom Project, and exchange letters with an incarcerated individual who is also working through the book. You can visit unconditionalfreedom.org/penpal to sign up. The back of this book provides more information about this program to better help you decide how you would like to proceed. We've seen each of these ways work, and no way is better than another. Do what speaks to you, not what anyone says is the way to do it.

We wish you luck. We wish you great forgiveness for all the mistakes you will make along the way, just as we have offered it to ourselves.

# INTRODUCTION

### The Way It Is

*There's a thread you follow. It goes among things that change.*
*But it doesn't change.*

~William Stafford

There are those of us who love—God, soul, spirit, Higher Power, Creator, or whatever you call it—in the depths of our being, but are not able to fit into conventional garb or a more common identity that would grant us this access. We are too wild, too feral, too opinionated, too bossy, too drunk, too much to be invited into the silent sanctums and pristine halls where traditional spirituality dwells. For much of my life I asked, *What is wrong with me?* It was the underlying question I dare not speak, even to myself. On the ladder, angels are both ascending and descending. There is a world of doctrine about how to ascend, which we see in religion, "chasing God," or other such rule-based, upward-looking pursuits. This book, however, shows how to descend, to incarnate. Those who are descending already know the spiritual truths. They have lived and studied religion with a rational, rule-driven mind, but in this life are learning to be human.

Many of us have wondered, *What is wrong with me? Why can't I just keep it together like other people? Those women who can be so demure, so polite, so capable of coloring inside the lines properly. Why do I always feel I need to cross over those lines? When other people stop—eating, flirting, loving, speaking—why does it seem I am just getting started? What is this irrepressible urge in me to know for myself and not just take the word—be it common sense, scripture, or cultural norm—that something is inherently good or evil, dark or light? Why do I feel the need to design from scratch, reinvent the wheel? Why can't I just buy off the rack?*

I remember listening to a New York City renaissance punk folk singer: "I'd rather throw beer than drink it, make art than buy it," and thinking, *That's it! I love the dirty-hands process of life, the coming to know, the intimacy.*

I tried everything from yoga to psychedelics, from academia to romance. The truth is, there was a wound inside of me that, if the wind blew the wrong way, burned with such white-hot flames that I feared I was being seared from the inside. There was positively no way to describe the uncomfortable feeling of the skin I lived inside. I tried more, from Sylvia Plath to Goth music. There was no salve. The only relief was when, on rare occasions, something beyond my control cracked me into a kind of abandon. It was as if my soul could come out of its tiny cell and roam. It devoured whatever it encountered, starved for love, for attention, for contact, for an experience, in the viscera of the eternal. Of the mystery. Of life. Of God. Of me, without the ideas chaining me to who I thought I should be to get love, attention, contact—in order to deserve the peace of the eternal, the sanctuary of God. Strife and effort, mostly directed at keeping that which was within me from breaking out of me, and into the world, marked my every move. If I had a path, it would have simply been, "constrict until you explode." Lose it. Try to clean up the damage. Constrict again.

I live making amends to that girl/woman who I once was. She is in each and all of us, rattling the cage. But to be honest, she is in some of us more than others. Some were born with more restless, agitated souls, souls that cannot merely lie down and be good animals in the petting zoo. We need to either be free, or we snarl and snap.

I keep a copy of this Liz Gilbert quote: "Great horses are not often easy horses. They have big egos and idiosyncrasies and quirks and foibles. Horses of a lifetime do exist, but only for riders who are skillful, tactful and courageous so that they can unlock the brilliance of their equine partners."

You may have been on such a horse. I was once on the difficult side of the horse, until I met someone who saw inside my wild—something beautiful, a potential. A person who did not say, "Tone it down, slow down, fit in."

Instead, they said, "You are magnificent precisely as you are." Not, "You will be great when you transform or get better," but, "You are a stunning creature now."

I would repeat those exact words to you if the circumstances were appropriate. I would have said that something is not *wrong* with you, something is *right* with you—beyond the pale of what the world can, for the most part, meet. People in bondage want people in bondage. Free people want free people. But very few people are free.

We would not be writing here were it not for the fact that imagining this world is too much to bear—a world where you either withdrew into a shell, into drugs and alcohol, into performance and pretending, a world where the real beauty was covered with counterfeit, a world where someone of such a gift would potentially take herself out of that pain. I am not writing a sanctimonious letter from on high. I've been all of it: suicidal, depressed, on welfare, not sure where my next paycheck would come from. I've sold my soul for love and acceptance. I've been in boatloads of trouble. Don't worry, I am not saying that the way I've discovered to grow my soul will bring you happiness. That has brought me to the depth of a despair I could not communicate anyway.

I stood once in Yerba Buena Gardens like a crazy woman. I prayed, *God, if this is it then take me. If not, show me.* But on that day, I was handed a thread. That thread led me into my own soul, where I could begin the real and only work there is: that of making an abode within my own soul that shelters me from the circumstances of this life. I get to experience the elements wild and alive, and I am free from the belief that any circumstance has power over me.

In other words, for better or worse, I own my own soul.

## Who We Are

We are soulmakers who invite you to join us. Our calling is to change ourselves into artists, masters of living and creating and loving. And in this fashion, we change the world. We discover our calling through the practices described in this book, and we turn more and more people on to their own voices, the masters inside of them, from whom we all long to hear. As each soul sings its newly discovered song, we believe a music will rise with a power not unlike the earth's bubbling core.

In soulmaking, we liberate the "stuck" energy that occurs as pain and suffering, transmuting it through creativity into the gold of power and vision, creation and love. We want you to learn that you are perfect in all your imperfection, that you are here to love and be loved, no matter what.

You will be, as Jung says, doing the only work there is to do, to make the unconscious conscious so that it no longer comes at you as "fate," and you can see a new resourcefulness, a means for turning insoluble problems into obstacles as in a game. Life is an endless series of obstacles that the resourceful mind sees as an opportunity to develop complexity, strength, resilience, empathy, and self-realization. The preconscious mind sees obstacles as a cause for defeat and defeatism, hopelessness, and collapse. This book demonstrates the procedures necessary to shift the organizing principle of one's mind from the lead of fate to the philosopher's stone that can turn every experience to gold, either a potent lesson or an aligned result.

Alchemy, the pursuit of turning base metals into gold, began as a chemical science in the Middle Ages, an impossible feat, but a process intended to create a transformation in its practitioners. Through the centuries, the word came to mean a magical transformation or creation, as in "I started singing one day, and it changed everything, converting a painful memory into a moving story." Alchemy is to soulmaking as concrete is to construction; you'll use it again and again and again.

As you work on your interior castle, you see that it is literally how you *see* that shifts your world; you grow a kind of 3D lens that can see through illusion, see the essence of all things and, most importantly, the love behind all things.

But it is not light fare. The stone can and must be applied to what we would most shy away from, for this is where there is the greatest potential—in the dark spots, the addiction and jealousy, the regret and the rage that we can mine the unmined and access the rawest power. Here we can draw ourselves back from all the ways we have accommodated or performed or pretended to be something other than who we are and, as a result, reclaim the hidden power of who we are.

We have heard that monks, after forty years of meditation, come up with a single conclusion: At the center of the heart lies beauty, truth, and love. I can confirm in my trek through the worst neighborhoods, not just mountaintops, but literal and figurative ghettos, that this is the case. When we explore our interior life, we remove the film from our eyes that manifests as fear or hatred, self-preservation or "playing a part" in our own lives. Here is where you either split from yourself to conform, or get cut off from the world. Here you fragment, blow apart, twist, and become deformed by what is not you.

# GENIUS IS YOUR CALLING

W̶e tend to think of a genius as a person who solves the world's most complex math problems or writes beautiful songs. But genius is a force, not a person. One person can demonstrate the force of genius in one moment, and not in the other. Albert Einstein had non-genius moments, and Michael Jordan was just a so-so baseball player. Genius is a force that passes through us, like love or compassion. We prepare our bodies and soften our minds, to open them to access genius. And then we wait. We do not own it; it does not belong to us, but it is our birthright.

When our genius is born, we look superhuman. The people who have found their genius can do the unimaginable, hear the inaudible, and see the invisible. They may look "crazy," but being fully crazy in a crazy world is being a pioneer. It is only here that we are granted our genius card. We are no longer constrained by artificial impediments and boundaries.

Genius uses what it has—an understanding of mathematical principles or a brush and paint, or even a plastic bucket to keep rhythm on—to transform energy into an object of beauty or something of use. Genius directs the purpose and aim of our existence; it's the energy that drives us to create, express, move, beget, forgive, and invent.

For centuries, human beings have used a "retreat" experience for self-reflection to contribute to a larger society. Removed from worldly pursuits and problems, the experience of solitude becomes an opportunity for self-reflection, meditation, and liberation. This is fertile ground for the force of genius to enter and instill its sense of purpose to heal ourselves and society.

Few people have time to retire to the monastery, but we can teach you to bring the monastery inside yourself. Build your own, as Saint Teresa said; create an "interior castle" that allows you to meet life on life's terms, without withdrawing, without denial, without fear.

The clarity and access to one's interior world that can be gained from this kind of extended period of self-reflection proves a great asset to society. Inner strength, commitment to genius, and self-knowledge begin to inform your outward actions. As you become more yourself, you become freer inside. New ideas are suddenly flowing in. We call that new energy Eros and it's here to drive you toward the reason we are all alive: creation. Love. Emotion rises and falls and moves you into new worlds where you could not go before, worlds you may have been too afraid to enter.

Say you are living a normal life in a suburban home and holding a job. All of your life you have had a bad temper, and on occasion this temper has gotten you into trouble. It's caused strain in your friendships, led to reckless driving—once, you even smashed a vase on the wall. You notice how, over the years, this once-innocent temper is growing increasingly threatening. Who do you want to talk to about this problem? Would it be someone who intellectually understands anger, the mechanics under which it operates, but does not live themselves bucked by its throes? Or would it be someone who's been to hell and back with their anger, has seen its worst and, having done the work of examining their interior world, has also seen its best?

At times, the guidance of our genius may encourage us to make confusing turns against what we've always done or were taught is "good." We may feel lost, neglected, or betrayed when genius asks us to pursue a course of action that contradicts our plans. But if we can trust this wisdom, we will always be directed to the center point of our true nature, to the core of our holiness, our "interior castle," and we will cultivate the ability to express that divinity under all conditions, along the way.

Consider Caravaggio, a violent, easily offended man who lived more than 500 years ago and heard the call to paint. He was in and out of jail constantly for various troubles and, fleeing his home after an attempted murder charge, continued to paint on the run.

*"I think everything in life is art. What you do. How you dress. The way you love someone, and how you talk. Your smile and your personality. What you believe in, and all your dreams. The way you drink your tea. How you decorate your home. Or party. Your grocery list. The food you make. How your writing looks. And the way you feel. Life is art."*

~HELENA BONHAM CARTER

He painted Bible scenes, but his genius spoke differently than other painters of the day. His holy subjects were depicted with gritty realism, not unlike the inside of a prison or a dark alley; light rakes across the figures as if streaming in through a small opening. His models were people he met on the street. *Death of the Virgin* used a drowned prostitute as the figure of Mary and when the painting arrived at the Vatican, a scandalized pope returned it.

Caravaggio's genius was the ability to draw in all his experience, all the darkness he'd seen and felt, and transform it with paint, no matter his circumstance. His life was often chaotic, full of poverty and rage, but his canvases were carefully planned out. Why was this seemingly "crazy" man driven to such expression?

His scenes were not "pretty," but they were powerful, heart-breaking, and heartfelt. His genius gave dignity to the silent lives of millions; in Caravaggio's eyes, a saint could resemble a common man. He converted anger, pain, isolation, and impulse into visions that now hang in the great churches and museums of the world. And no matter where he was or how fast he was running, he painted. Caravaggio accepted what he was and where he was, and he fully engaged with his calling. He instinctively used alchemy—changing pain into beauty, connecting deeply with his genius, and changing the course of Western art.

*Genius has no inhibitions. When in its thrall, we lose all sense of time, place, and space while creating.*

## You Have Genius

The clarity and access to one's interior world that can be gained from this kind of soulmaking proves a great asset to society. Who better to help heal wounds and injustice than those who have traveled to the edges of it, who know its outer bounds and perhaps beyond?

## A Caution as You Enter This Path

What we are describing is a difficult path. We can always continue in old ways, claiming superior spiritual ideals and praying desperately that wild forces inside do not reappear. But this new path asks us to name our pain and grief and rage, examine it, and become friends with all of it. Learn to work with our pain and release it through the art we make and the art of our life. On those terms, these feelings become our power—fierce, loyal, and most importantly, harnessed—for building, creating, connecting, and growing.

---

Spirituality, secular or religious, is a serious enterprise with potentially perilous consequences. For all who dare venture into the true 'spiritual' realm—the passionate, shadowy domain of the daimons—must be psychologically and emotionally prepared to meet the metaphorical dark deities, forces, powers or spirits, abandoning all hope, as Dante forewarned, of finding only friendly, benign or benevolent ones. Many seekers, alas, are not.

Herein lies a common recipe for spiritual disaster . . . In the final analysis, the fundamental task of a secular spiritual psychology is to redeem (rather than cast out or exorcize) our devils and demons. It is inevitably both a psychological and spiritual venture. Psychotherapy such as this is one way of coming to terms with the daimonic. By bravely voicing our inner "demons"—symbolizing those unconscious tendencies we most fear, flee from, and hence, are obsessed or haunted by—we transmute them into helpful spiritual allies, in the form of newly liberated, life-giving psychic energy, for use in constructive activity. During this process, the strange paradox that many artists and spiritual savants embrace is discovered: That same devil so righteously run from and rejected turns out to be the redemptive source of vitality, creativity, and authentic spirituality.

—Stephen Diamond, "Psychotherapy, Evil, and the Daimonic: Toward a Secular Spiritual Psychology," in *Spirituality and Psychological Health*.

# WELCOME TO
## *THE ART OF SOULMAKING*

---

T his world of the soul is different from the world of the spirit. The world of the spirit is filled with those who may see themselves "enlightened." Often misunderstood or downright shamed, people who live in the world of the soul get their hands and faces dirty. In the world of the soul, there is no such thing as eternal damnation, and there is no such thing as a life wasted.

With the world of only "spiritual" teachings, you work *for* them; you learn them with your mind. With the soul, you often get cracked wide open by feeling and intuition, and a "knowing" floods your being. Spiritual teachings instruct you to forgive someone because it is the right thing to do. With the soul, you do the treacherous work of remaining in tune with your heart, letting all your messy, conflicting feelings have space to breathe, trusting that the process of remaining true to oneself will end in a noble result. You do it because it *feels* right inside of you. Just try it. Forgive, really forgive by embracing an "enemy" and feel it. You know it's right because the sensation of forgiving is that of becoming freer, more alive. You no longer have a negative emotion drawing down your energy source.

In this soul-world, the interior world softens, the heart softens, you begin to hear a deeper wisdom as your presence carves out space for compassion and empathy for others too. You are naturally drawn to forgive the judgmental person who spoke to you harshly or the neighborhood kid who bullied you, because your compassionate heart understands they were simply doing their best.

In the world of the spiritual, prisons, bad neighborhoods, and all the "dark places" must be avoided at all costs, because they will distract from the true destination of pristine cleanliness. The "light spaces"—the sacred temples and gleaming high rises—exist as superior to the dark places. We question this fixation with the "light" in the spiritual world. It presents a lopsided view of what life is and what life requires. The darkness, we say, holds many lessons, many gifts. In the world of the soul, the darkness is where true change of the heart occurs. We must be willing and able to go there in ourselves and with others.

Darkness holds the wildness, the secrets, and all the states we attempt to hide; it hides our "shadow" as well. "Shadow" is a psychological term, which means a repressed or unacknowledged characteristic. The light is easy to see; the shadow is more elusive. Take for example the woman who dates many men, and scoffs at the lifestyle of married women. "I feel so bad for you that you have just one man," she says, with a tone that clearly shows how superior she feels about her single lifestyle.

But in this case, the married woman is quite happy. Most people who know both women would say the married one is even happier than the single woman. She has a fulfilling marriage, rich with intimacy, real vulnerability, and trust. You hear the single woman touting her judgment, while in your gut you know that she's just envious. She won't admit that she's envious; she can't. She can only express her envy as superiority and ridicule. She can't express envy because she literally can't "see" it, she can't acknowledge it. At least not yet. It's in her shadow. This married woman carries the shadow of the single woman; she represents her repressed desire to settle down, to go deep with just one partner.

The "spiritually superior" individual will isolate what they cannot control. They shiver at the "other" who does not look and speak like they do; they fear each other, and they fear themselves, what they are capable of if they lose control. They live behind bars they built for themselves, and they do not hear what you will hear; they have not made the commitment and they are not called. Make no mistake, there is a way to approach all your experience—happy, horrifying, rich, or desperately impoverished—as your calling, your soul work.

Part One of your initiation is to choose to accept your position no matter where you are. If you are on the top of the mountain, do you fear the mountain will fall? If you've lost everything you ever had, can you face the derision and abandonment? Your initiation is to take it, and not take it personally. Soul gives the toughest battles to the strongest soldiers.

Part Two is to forgive, to release any claim to repayment for what has happened to you, and the resentment for any hurt you have received during this trip called life. You can clear your heart of hatred and blame and send any poison you have taken in back out as love. That's soulmaking and it changes *everything*.

The following is an extreme example, but an empowering one to share. A man seemingly at the bottom of existence became one of our great soul teachers.

This friend is a pen pal on death row. We chose to write to him because of all the letters we read, his letter demonstrated that he had eyes to see. Every other letter, and we read thousands, contained the sentence, "I am not supposed to be here."

We understand that what everyone goes through in such a place is a process, much like wailing over the dead is a part of grief. This is to be expected. But his guilt or innocence was of no interest to us; it was a straw man that breaks apart with the slightest breeze. What matters was, what was he going to do with this experience right now? It is the same question wherever you are; can you see a higher power in the center of the experience? If you are not guilty, take every legal step to get out. But for present purposes, you are here now. What will you make of this life?

The incarcerated individual we chose was the one who said, "I am here." He communicated a profound acceptance. In initiation, the answer to every prayer is acceptance; acceptance is freedom, rather than giving in.

He told a story of how in prison, everyone suggested that he become a Christian because Christians are more likely to get time off their sentences and enjoy liberties others don't. It was a well-known scam. He may be incarcerated, he said, but he could not pretend to be something he was not. He had not, in fact, ever heard or felt God. It would have been a lie to say he had.

Then one night while he was lying on his bunk in his cell, he felt a presence. He did hear a voice. And clear as day, the voice told him that he could be free right where he was if he would help others, right where he was. He feared he had nothing to offer but was "told" that if he just said yes, he would be given the power. He said yes. He could not say if it was Jesus or any particular form of God, he only knew in his bones that what he heard was real. That he could trust.

He simply started looking for where others were in need. He listened to the guy whose wife decided she couldn't take his being in prison and was filing for divorce. He listened to the guy who got a cancer diagnosis and was going to die in prison. He showed up for the guy who got the crap kicked out of him. He was no expert, he just showed up. He released his hatred of the correctional officers and slowly, very slowly, built a rapport of civility. He understood they too were answering their call and executing it at times with grace, at times with cruelty, but that his work was to answer to the judge within his heart.

The next thing he knew, guys were lining up to talk to him. He didn't know how, but he knew the right thing to say. Something inside him woke up, a kind of knowing that went beyond him. One day he realized that he was totally free, right where he was. He realized he was freer than he ever was on the outside, and freer than anyone he'd ever met. He was granted a peace beyond human understanding. He realized that wherever he was, if his body were to be set free tomorrow, he would simply continue to do the same thing. So he stopped fighting.

He realized that he was posted to this station because he "could" be. He had what it took, a conviction about who he was, an unwillingness to pretend, an honesty. And this made him the perfect candidate to be the master of this location (although he might not have called himself such).

This man taught us much about the workings of life that cannot be learned from the great texts or in protected "safe" environments. He had in-the-field training and an experiential compassion that felt otherworldly. Corresponding with him, we had the intuitive sense that he would flinch at nothing we could share with him. There was no aspect of our lives, our beliefs, that he would reject—not because he was so high, so distanced from it, but because the profound depth of acceptance he carved out, in his own life, extended to everyone he met.

Because he was so "low," he had lived through worse experiences than most people around him and had room to receive them. His was a most intimate compassion. This is what the realization of the soul looks like—where you go from theoretical ideas of what being "good" means, to actual experience. Soulmaking is parallel to the ancient Greek idea of *agape*, love turned into action.

Our friend lived in a literal prison; most people do not. They live in cages with invisible bars they made themselves; a woman inside an unhappy home cannot bear what others will say about her, should she leave. A man who once dreamed of being a pilot sits at a desk for thirty years, only to die of a heart attack twenty minutes after lunch one day. He never navigates the sky before returning to earth.

We all face the horrors of our own mind, but can we remain conscious here? Can we hold true to the values in our heart here? Under the most heinous duress? When everything in you is reduced to survival, to self-preservation, when you are being mistreated—can you offer yourself there? In these dark environments are the last test and proof of one's conviction: here where there is no room for lofty ideas.

Our friend realized that wherever he was, if his body were to be set free tomorrow, he would still be the same man he was right now, in his cell. That's what we mean by soulmaking. Meet the moment, no matter how bad—or good—it is.

Like our pen pal friend, at first you can deny your situation, fight it, and make it wrong. You have free will. But this will not do what this initiation is here to do, and that is to free your soul from any condition whatsoever. And in the process, become someone who, by your very existence, frees others.

From here, we cannot describe the beauty of the world that emerges. To have nothing but truth move you. To see all the nakedness of emperors. To be granted X-ray vision. To be able to love as much as the human heart wants to—even the prisoners and wardens of the world. To welcome them all.

This course is about the journey into the inner workings of your soul. Soulmaking.

Unconditional freedom is that field. There is no right and wrong here; no political conservative against Black activists; no Left, no Right; no camps, no guards. Here you are free.

We recognize the very things you believe are wrong with you—your history, your failings, your mental health problems, your obsessions, your fanaticism and your mania, your fear and your loneliness—prequalify you for soulmaking. Pain, complexity, rage, joy, and everything in between move inside of you; all the elements of soulmaking are there. We're here to teach you how to use these forces to connect and create—the reason we are alive.

A person in prison meditates in a cell that becomes an inner monastery for transformation; a musician hiding from soldiers reimagines the sound of gunshots into a guitar solo; a painter paints her own horrific accident again and again; a mother writes in her kitchen alone, long into the night; an architect builds a cathedral over a slave pit; a composer turns weeping into a song. Magicians all, they seek their truth no matter the constraints of society's boundaries and laws. In the process, their craft of taking the very pain in front of them and transforming this pain to an offering to society transforms them.

A word we'll use throughout this course to describe this process is *alchemy*. We've all heard of this before in our culture: Making lemonade from lemons. Turning lead into gold. In soulmaking, you use alchemy for your soul. Think of the victim who forgives her transgressor and the two create a theater show about forgiveness, reaching thousands with their message; or the husband and

*"Out beyond ideas of wrongdoing and rightdoing there is a field. I'll meet you there. When the soul lies down in that grass the world is too full to talk about."*

~RUMI

wife who lose a biological child and decide to adopt two more who'd otherwise grow up in orphanages. In both examples, they took great pain and forged it into love; they made the world *better*.

We invite you to become the alchemist of your own experiences, your own heart. Your obstacles, setbacks, heartbreaks, and losses become pure gold. Pain transforms into something beautiful, something that connects us to one another, something of use. You become crazy-wise, converting all that has touched you into a nonrational approach of soul and applying it, with rigor, to the practical, rational world of science, consciousness practices, and social change.

# THE SOULMAKER MOVEMENT: PRINCIPLES

---

### Reunion: Wholeness Requires the Individual

The work of the individual is to know the whole of creation. To do so, we orient ourselves around the truth and seek to harmonize the deepest expression of our unique blueprint with the whole of creation. When we bind ourselves to the inward image of our soul, to our blueprint, and fully express who we essentially are, that expression will draw us into ever-deepening intimacy with our environment, with nature, with others around us. We know ourselves by knowing the world, and we know the world by knowing ourselves; in doing so, we unite heaven and earth, below and above, within and without.

### Alchemy: Convert the Smog of the World into Oxygen

Our work is to draw in the war of the world, the pain, and radiate it back out as love. Because we can no longer see ourselves as separate from the world, we relate to the pain and the war of the world as an externalized reflection of our inward state. We purify ourselves by loving that which our conditioning would see as distasteful in the world. The alchemical process of individuation requires us to direct our attention to light up within. By doing this, we transform "lead" into "gold" and from there, we can covert the smog of the world into oxygen.

### Circulation: Fill What Is Empty and Empty What Is Full

Our focus and path are love, and our means is circulation. A healthy heart keeps energy circulating throughout the body and in the world. In alchemy, this is referred to as the *circulatio,* in which the material is repeatedly dissolved, sublimated, and coagulated. We fill what is empty, and empty what is full.

### Co-creation: The Bee and the Flower Are Equally Benefiting

We recognize the mutuality of existence as connected beings and do the work to develop the capacity to both transmit and receive energy. The bee transmits pollen and receives nectar. In the process, the bee gets sustenance and the flower gets to reproduce; both are equally receiving. All persons are caught in an inescapable network of mutuality, tied into a single garment of destiny. Whatever affects one directly, affects all indirectly. As in: "I can never be what I ought to be until you are what you ought to be, and you can never be what you ought to be until I am what I ought to be." Co-creation is a reciprocal process where everyone benefits. Together we build an entire ecology. We are all in this together.

### Meeked-ness: The Meeked Shall Inherit the Earth

We believe the "meeked" shall inherit the earth. The ancient Greek word for meek, *praus* (πραεῖς), was used to refer to a horse trained for battle. Wild stallions were captured for riding, pulling, and general labor. For these horses, it was essential that their wild nature be broken. Of those horses, there was a set that, despite the best training, always retaining a part of that wild nature. These horses were trained, disciplined, and obedient, but never broken. They were unconditional. The stallion that is the "meeked" one, retaining his wild nature, is the most obedient to the unalterable truth. Meeked is reserved for the strongest among us. For when the strongest are obedient to unalterable truth, they can endure the weight of compassion and open-heartedness.

### Remembrance: Remember to Remember

We already know. Our only work is to remember. And then to remember to remember. When the situation is the most challenging, we remember to remember. We leave reminders at the door of consciousness to get back to our bodies and retain the beginner's mind over and over. To "remember to remember" is to remember to seek *anamnesis*—to remember to go inward and recover what we've always already known.

### Incarnation: Build the New That Makes the Old Obsolete

The purpose of life is not to ascend, but to incarnate—to draw heaven down to earth. As such, we must become good stewards of our inheritance. To do this, we evoke our heirloom humanity through the process of re-wilding. We allow our nature to take over, heal itself, and grow freely. That is how we turn corn back into maize. Our task is to remember the wisdom of our soul and reshape the world through the expression of that wisdom. We came here to infuse the material world with spirit, to incandesce the world. From here we build the new that makes the old obsolete.

### Cultivation: Bring Forth What Is Within You (Gospel of St. Thomas)

Our journey is to become the artist who can bring forth the truths of the human soul with exquisite beauty. "If you bring forth what is within you, what you bring forth will save you. If you do not bring forth what is within you, what you do not bring forth will destroy you." There is union between spirit and soul. We meet in that location. We welcome the daimon that is equal parts destruction and creation and believe that which is not integrated is exaggerated.

### Play: Potential Is Discovered in Play

Potential is realized in play. In the words of Maslow, we've focused enough on the ailment. It is time to focus on the potential; that is what we aim to do through converting the "negative" stagnation into potential and using it according to each person's desire. We find this while in a state of play. The world and all its trauma is not a hell-realm to be overcome, but a playground to be made love to. To seek freedom in all conditions is to drop

ourselves into uncomfortable positions and see how we can infuse those conditions with levity, spontaneity, and play and allow
ourselves to be surprised by our own creative responses and resourcefulness. By changing the stakes, the one who plays allows
for possibility, uncovers hidden talents, and lives in their genius.

### Purposefulness: Your Pain Is Your Purpose

Our pain is our purpose. To harvest the fruits of our pain, it is
not enough to merely heal. It is our unique calling, our path. Our
pain thus becomes the path to our greatness. We turn poison into
medicine.

### Rehumanizing: We Are Inestimably Powerful

We recognize the inestimable power of each and begin each conversation, both personal and cultural, as such. We do not need
to find Oz in order to have brains, heart, and courage. We merely
need to remind ourselves the power is already inside of us. We
are already home. Those who society has marginalized—the imprisoned, the mentally ill, the homeless, the crazy ones—have the
most unexplored potential. The only option is to learn how to
work with them in such a way as to turn lead into gold and see
what the "wild ones" may have to teach us. In "rehumanizing" the
marginalized, we unlock the power of the world.

### Unconditionality: Freedom in All Conditions

We aim for unconditional love, Eros, freedom, and truth without
exception. Each of us must be trained in unconditional freedom;
how to find meaning and purpose right where we are. This creates resilient, kind, present, resourceful, playful human beings.
We approve of all conditions, both internal and external, that create barriers to full expression. Obstacles are the path—freedom
beyond circumstance, in all conditions.

### Eudaimonia: Unique Blueprint Leads to Human Flourishing

*Eudaimonia* is the notion that within each of us is a unique
blueprint or calling, that when expressed, leads us to a state of

flourishing. This in turn brings the precise, vital nutrient the world is missing. Einstein said, "If you judge a fish by its ability to climb a tree, it will always look stupid." We believe in judging each person by the metrics of their arena. To use generalized measurements of "value" and "worth" to people robs them from developing and expressing their uniqueness and leaves us with a culture lacking what genius would contribute.

### Synthesis: Genius Is Found in Synthesis
Eros is the union of opposites into a bigger whole. Genius is found in synthesis, the marriage of opposites. We recognize the space that separates us can connect us. The unions of light and dark, good and bad, rational and nonrational, open up a third path. This marriage between the letter of the law and spirit of the law gives birth to a higher truth.

### Pacify: Emanate a Spirit of Peace to a Turbulent World
We reinstate flow when circulation is constricted. To pacify is to send in Eros, the unifying spirit, when someone feels agitated or out of alignment. Emanate a pacifying energy; radiate it. We trust that holding our own interior calm in an increasingly shaken world is the maker of harmony.

### Collective: The Next Leader Will Be the Collective
The collective will transform the world. When we as a community inhabit the spirit of Eros, the community itself becomes the leader. From here, we serve the numinous instead of the numinous serving us.

### Reception: True Power Is That of Reception
True power, like gravity, is the power of reception that converts the repugnant into the desirable. What if we were the answer to the question of our time, Will you receive me? Will you receive me unconditionally, without judgment or agenda? We believe in the taking in of the whole world, the way one would make love to the whole of the world.

## Our Mission

Our mission is to transform hearts and open minds. In doing so, we seek to convert a judgmental, closed society into a community of open, conscious individuals who place the ultimate value on creativity, truth, connection, and love. We seek unconditional freedom where the self is never chained, no matter the outward circumstances.

Our method uses the examined interior life to effect change on the exterior. Heal thyself and heal the world; connect to thyself and connect to the world; free thyself, free the world; serve thyself by serving the world.

### Why We Do What We Do

Our experience is that life is purposeful. Purposeful in that we are all here to make our unique contribution to society. There is living "in your life," and there is living "out of your life." Either can happen anywhere and at any time.

"Living in your life" is living with a purpose. You are emotionally available, and you exist in an interchange with the people around you, where you are enriched by your environment, just as your environment enriches you. Life is deepening over time. "Living out of your life" looks like denial, self-consciousness, distraction, and refusing to digest the emotional content of your life. "In" is heaven; "out" is hell. "In" can happen in a prison cell just as easily as "out" can happen in a cathedral. Your environment does not dictate your life.

True healing in the world will arise not from the completion of a battle of ideas, but rather from a group of people who agree to live *in* their life.

# SPIRIT VERSUS SOUL

A brief overview of John Tarrant's seminal *The Light Inside the Dark* (1998) divides our consciousness into "spirit" and "soul," opposing poles that work in tandem to make a whole human being.

"Spirit" is transparent, and it is given. It cannot be produced by focusing on it; one must grow quiet and uncover it. It is our tie to a vast eternity, a stillness where there is no content. Spirit is where you were born, and where you shall return. Connecting to it requires a practice: meditation, prayer, and the long, slow process of letting go that drops us into a place where the still center comes into view. When we make contact with it, we understand there is no beginning and no end. We are what came before, and we are what will come again.

Spirit is the purview of religions, where the rules are clear and ordered. With spirit, our life here is clearly seen and shines down in all directions. Yet alone, spirit is weak, too clear about its goals, reckless and headlong in its pursuit of them. Spirit is too full of absolutes. Alone, it cannot engage with the unpredictable, delicious, heartbreaking joy known as life.

At the other pole is "soul," a dirty-faced, beaming actor full of sound and fury, gasping and laughter. Soul bubbles up from below where the wildness lives; it is always trying to embrace things, inhabiting the brokenness of the world. Soul is creative: it produces something out of matter. It's how we connect with others and feel less lonely in tangible human ways.

Soul loves to live and learn; it is always trying to embrace things. It brings meaning to experience, including the thoughtful aspects of our being. It throws its arms around what we know most dimly of ourselves or sometimes shudder at: hidden passions and insomnia; helpless, almost indestructible longings, obsession, ruminations, and secrets; and the continuing under-current of knowledge that some losses are irretrievable. Soul is the gift that makes us less perfect, so that we can be more whole.

Having one without the other creates a misshapen interior. Without the positive and negative charges of soul and spirit, consciousness, like molecules, falls to pieces. By moving be-tween the two—a cycling between the white light of spirit and the darker earthier depths of soul—the organism is brought back into balance. We are complete. If spirit is too dominant, long-repressed natural appetites become swollen and explode with tragic consequences. Soul left to its own devices is a Bugatti racer with no brakes.

Employed together, a pleasing tension arises between spirit and soul. Rational thought and wild creativity flourish in the same organism quite peacefully.

If spirit is represented by light and lives in the mind, soul emanates from the body and is charged with a wild eroticism that drives creation. Put them together, and learn what it feels to be complete.

# PART I

# CLEARING YOUR BUILDING SITE

Building a stronger refuge where the soul can live requires that we clear the "land" inside of ourself. During the first half of this program, we hope you will sink down into your past, exploring the strong places as well as the weaker ones.

# ONE ACRE OF LAND

To paraphrase writer Anne Lamott, imagine that every newborn is given an acre of land. That acre represents what she will grow and nurture in this life; except this acre is our soul, the spot where we build our life. We can grow what we love: tomatoes, watermelon, spinach, and apples, or allow weeds to choke out the bodybuilding foods, leaving nothing but bitter leaves and poisonous berries.

There's a gate on one side of your acre. You get to choose who gets inside and who must stay out; that is a huge part of life. Who are you letting inside? Once in, what do they do? Are they creators or destroyers? This choice is as important as the plants you put in your dirt.

Farm your acre with great care. Touch the soil with your hands. Is it hydrated, and well tilled? Does it feel dry, deserted? Either way, this is your plot. You only have one on which to build a life. Value, feeling good about yourself, and purpose all grow from this acre. In the end, that's what you cultivate.

# MORNING PRACTICE

## How to Work Your Acre: Introduction to Morning Practice

M orning Practice is a daily tending to our soil. This is a base from which everything else grows. The care and attention you put inside determines what comes out of you.

Morning practice can be enjoyable at times, something to look forward to. Other days, it may seem like a drag. This is no different than any other kind of mastery; they all involve dedication. Monks sit in meditation daily, no matter their mood. NBA players practice millions of layups and pivots before they take it outside. Both will tell you: The less you want to do it, the more you need to do it. They practice their genius relentlessly. They bring to practice their problems, frustration, and pains. Their practice becomes a sacred space that is only theirs, where slowly they begin to trust, transform, and master their game.

Practice is about disrupting autopilot. This precious time opens you up to receive the deeper truths often masked by your own negative thought loops, intense emotions, and other people's comments. You will come to look forward to the repetitive nature, the ritual of your morning, and receiving its fresh energy and new insights into you and your life. Practice is about becoming so still you can hear the voices inside you, your intuition, your North Star.

In this section are instructions for yoga, a daily Soul Inventory, and a seated meditation. The yoga postures, or *asanas*, help invigorate the body and provide energy for the day. A Soul Inventory helps you get to know yourself on a deeper level, as you will often discover things you did not expect. This is where you are

**Life is a practice. To gain skill at anything, you must do it and then do it again, over and over, to gain confidence and mastery. The more skillful you become, the more life you live. Commit to this practice just as you would a fitness regime because that's what it is, a workout to strengthen your soul.**

going to carve out the temple of your soul. Meditation reduces stress, develops concentration, and opens you to connect with your own deeper wisdom and creativity.

Each practice can stand alone, but we strongly recommend you commit to at least one hour per day. Here is a possible structure:

1. 10 minutes of yoga;
2. 10 minutes of writing a Soul Inventory; and
3. 10 minutes of seated meditation.

Start with ten minutes and build upward to twenty, if it feels better. Your target is one hour a day of soulmaking, just for you. This hour is your sacred space, the spot where you begin building your interior monastery.

## Yoga

The main thing to remember about yoga is to listen to your body above all. If something is painful, ease up. If something feels great and you want to go deeper, feel free. Begin the conversation with your body; you'll find it a good and wise companion. The body often opens when we relax, and constricts when we push, just like the mind.

One round of Sun Salutations is a series of twelve yoga poses that flow together in coordination with the breath. Their purpose is to warm up the body at the beginning of a yoga session before practicing individual poses. Beginning yogis typically take ten minutes to do three rounds of Sun Salutations, which leaves ten minutes for relaxation at the end. The final relaxation is as important as the Sun Salutations. After you have learned this basic series, we offer more variations in later courses. Most importantly, have fun!

To start, come to a comfortable, cross-legged seated position. Place a pillow or a rolled-up blanket or sweatshirt underneath your hips. This way the hips are higher than the ankles, and you can sit more comfortably. Roll your pelvis slightly forward so you

can ground down through the front of your sitz bones—the ones
you sit on at that base of your pelvis. Hands can rest comfortably
on the knees, shoulders relaxed, chin parallel to the floor. Close
your eyes and take a couple of deep breaths here. Typical yoga
breathing is in through the nose and out through the nose. As you
breathe deeply into the abdomen, let the belly expand. Then as
you exhale, draw the belly button in toward your spine. Many of
us breathe the opposite of this pattern, so don't worry if it takes
some practice to get it.

Next, stand up with your feet parallel, hip-width's distance
apart. Knees above ankles. Hips above knees. Shoulders above
hips. Rock back and forth until you find your center from front
to back. Shift your weight side to side until you find your weight
equally distributed between right and left. Roll your shoulders
back and down. Keep your hands by your sides. Palms can be
facing forward. Chin parallel to the ground. Imagine someone
is pulling a string up from the crown of your head, lengthening
your spine.

Now move through the series, which is also called a "flow."

1.  Inhale. Then as you exhale, bring your palms together in front of your chest.

2.  Inhale again as you extend your arms out and up alongside your ears, palms facing each other. Take a gentle backward bend from just beneath the shoulders.

3.  Exhale, hinging forward into the Standing Forward Fold
    with a flat back, releasing and relaxing over the legs. Let
    the spine lengthen and the head hang. You can nod the
    head yes, shake the head no, relaxing and releasing all the
    muscles in the back of the neck. Place your hands flat on
    the floor on either side of the feet, fingertips in line with
    the toe tips. Bend your knees, if you need to, to get the
    palms flat on the floor.

4.  Inhale. Stretch the left leg far back and come into a Low
    Lunge. Your left knee comes down to the floor. Release the
    top of the left foot on the floor. Make sure the right knee
    stays directly above the right ankle. Your front shin should
    be perpendicular to the floor. If the knee goes past the
    front ankle, it can put too much stress on the knee joint.
    You can come up onto your fingertips. Lengthen out the
    back of the neck. Drop the pelvis down and stretch. (If you
    have any knee pain, place a blanket or pillow underneath
    that back knee.)

5.  Exhale to move into Downward Facing Dog (Down Dog for
    short). If you have a four-legged friend, you've probably
    seen them do this! Weight is distributed evenly between
    hands and feet. If you want to, take a few breaths here. You
    can alternate bending one knee and stretching the arch
    of that foot, and then straightening it when you bend the
    other knee and stretch the opposite arch. Do this a few
    times. Then bring your chest closer to the floor. Keep your
    ears in between your upper arms. Bend your knees and tilt
    the sitz bones up toward the sky. If at any point Down Dog
    becomes too intense, you can: a) put your forearms and
    elbows down on the ground instead of just your hands, or
    b) come down and rest in Child's Pose. To rest in Child's
    Pose, drop your knees, shins, and tops of the feet down to
    the floor and sit back on your heels with your arms stretch-
    ing out in front of you. Your forehead rests on the ground.
    Come back to Down Dog to transition into the next pose.

6. Bring your knees down to the floor, then chest down, then chin down. Keep the pelvis raised and toes tucked under. Elbows are close to the sides of the body.

7.  Press through the toes and slide the torso along the floor until your legs are straight. Inhale to come into Baby Cobra. Release the tops of the feet onto the floor. There is no weight in the palms. The head, neck, and chest are slightly lifting off the ground. Bring your awareness to your upper back. Imagine the shoulder blades are sliding down your back toward the base of your spine. Elbows stay close to the body. The back of your neck is long. Look up with your eyes.

8.  Inhale. Tuck the toes, press into the palms, lift the hips, and exhale into Down Dog.

9. Inhale. Bring your left foot forward in between the hands to come into Low Lunge on the other side. Let the right knee rest on the floor. (Again, if you have any knee pain, place a blanket or pillow underneath that back knee). Make sure your left knee stays directly above the left ankle. Drop your pelvis down while you lengthen your spine.

**10.** Exhale. Bring the right foot forward to meet the left, stand up, and then bow into Standing Forward Fold. Release and relax your head and neck. Imagine that your head is heavy like a bowling ball and completely let it go.

**11.** Inhale. Bring your arms up alongside your head. Hinge up with a flat back. Bend your knees if you need to, to protect your lower back. Take a gentle backward bend at the top of the inhalation from just beneath the shoulders.

12. Exhale. Palms together in front of the heart. Congratulations! You just completed your first round of Sun Salutations!

Now release the hands to the sides. Your feet remain hip distance apart. Close your eyes and observe the effects of your first round of Sun Salutations. Your heart might be beating slightly faster than before, your breath might have changed in some way, or you may feel a bit warmer. You may not notice anything at all. And that's okay too!

Repeat the Sun Salutation series (poses 1 to 12) two more times.

With practice, you will get the movement and breath pattern down and start to feel your own flow. Yoga is different from exercise. It is consciously moving in time with your breath and becoming aware of how you feel in each moment. Three rounds of Sun Salutations take about ten minutes and are a great way to start the day.

Most importantly, after you finish all three rounds of Sun Salutations, lie down on your back for Final Relaxation. Your feet should be about two to three feet apart. Your palms should be facing up, about a foot away from the sides of the body. Set a timer for ten minutes and relax here. This lets the body integrate the benefits from the Sun Salutations.

Of course, you can modify the pose so that it works for your body. If you have lower back pain, bend your knees and place your feet flat on the floor. Separate your feet wider than your hips, and let your knees rest against each other. You can do the Final Relaxation Pose with your knees bent.

## Soul Inventory

Once your body is open and warm from the yoga, take out a pad of paper and spend twenty minutes writing. Nothing is off-limits; this letter is for you and you alone.

A Soul Inventory is your soul's cannon; you are writing a doctrine on the way your soul wants to express itself. This is the place where you begin to meet yourself. This is a conversation, one that will continue your entire life. This is you speaking to your soul, and your soul speaking back to you. This is not about receiving guidance from High Above; this is about sinking in, speaking to the small, still animal inside of you. Guide the writing and let the writing guide you. This is what your soul wants to express.

Like prayer, soulmaking is a conversation and, as one rabbi put it, in prayer, God is a verb. Like all communication, if one speaks and no one is listening, it's not communication; it's noise. The connection between two or more, the golden thread that connects us all, of speaking and listening, listening and speaking, cannot be broken. Other verbs such as loving, sharing, dancing, and hugging are the same. Without the golden thread connecting two humans, the action—as well as the verb that describes it—no longer exists. There is no hug, no love, no God without the verb.

All of life is a verb because of the need to connect our thread to another soul. In this way, prayer becomes "God-ing." In human relationships, one person is wife-ing while the other is husband-ing in traditional roles in an endless loop of *Father Knows Best*. We are all verbs, Joan-ing and Mark-ing our way through the world, connected and in need of one another. As you Joan and Mark, you learn through the connection that we are all the same.

When Mother Teresa prayed, she spoke and she *listened*. As you develop your soulmaking, sit down to write. Ideas, emotions, and memories will come to you, seemingly from nowhere. Write it all down and as your inner castle forms, shapes become clearer. Each morning when you take up your writing, you meet your soul again in a never-ending conversation. As your journey goes deeper, you can revisit your younger "soulmaking self" and feel how far you've come—as well as how far you'd like to go.

All sky travelers, from pilots to astronauts, have gyroscopes and, because your soul is on its great journey, you will need one too. Gyroscopes show the *level* so that when planes bounce around in turbulence, the pilot can restore balance and continue to fly parallel to the ground. This is the instrument that keeps them from flying into mountains. In these pages, you'll become attuned to what you need to stay level as you go. No matter what jagged cliffs your soulmaking encounters, your gyroscope keeps you flying.

*"God speaks in the silence of the heart, and we listen. And then we speak to God from the fullness of our heart and God listens. And this listening and this speaking is what prayer is meant to be."*

~MOTHER TERESA

Your gyroscope will keep you safe as well. When you dip into intense internal or external situations, your inside alarm will tell you if you have strayed too far off your course. The gyroscope is implied in the answer a kabbalah teacher gave to the question: Can spiritual teachings be dangerous?

The teacher replied, "Only if you don't have a strong enough tether."

Consult your gyroscope often, or you may find yourself upside down, mid-flight.

Your one acre of land, your soul, the very dirt that makes you who you are is turned over and aerated each day as you write your inventory. In this way, you see and, more importantly, *feel* yourself, your energy, your desires, and your dreams. You can care for the abandoned spaces within yourself and release what no longer serves you. In this way, day by day, we make the soul and move toward unconditional freedom, no matter the circumstances in which we find ourselves.

Following are different soul exercises that will help you mine the gold inside: your genius, your soul. Use some and not others. Once again, this is about choice and what is most effective for you. As you move through the lessons of soulmaking, whenever you please, return here and use these techniques.

Sit down and start with this simple question: What wants to be heard and what wants to be said?

*Dreams*

A dream can be tricky, but the key is to pay attention to the different types of dreams you have. Some have messages, lessons, memories, premonitions, themes, or abstractions, and others may be a random expression of your subconscious. The more you pay attention, the more interesting you will find them. If you relive a certain memory, note it and how it may change in your mind as you dream it. Repetitive dreams of falling often represent fear; dreams of forgetting to wear clothes can represent insecurity. If you have a feeling upon waking, note that as well. Write about your dreams throughout this practice.

What role did you play in your dream? Were you the observer? The hero? Where were you in your dream? Describe the place. Were you indoors? Outdoors? In your family home? What did you feel while you were dreaming? How did you feel when you woke up?

## Automatic Writing

Automatic writing is the practice of writing words in a trance-like state that originates from outside conscious awareness. Psychologists and spiritualists have varying beliefs about the origin of automatic writing, with some arguing that it is sourced from the unconscious mind, and others claiming that it originates from supernatural forces such as spirit guides and angels.

Sit comfortably with your pen and paper. You can have your eyes open or closed, whichever helps you focus. Some days, stories will push up through your pen, as will thoughts and feelings you may or may not know you even had. Ask a question of the Universe or ask for help. If this doesn't work for you the first time, try it again. Practice requires repetition to receive its true benefits.

## Letting the Shadow Show Itself

Carl Jung, the founder of analytic psychology, advises careful investigation of our darkest desires and their motivations, and our childish fantasies and resentments, in order to be free of the past rather than haunted by it.

The gruesome monster in the church attic is afraid to be seen; he will be misunderstood, and no one will love him. A mother sits and writes down a ghost story about lost children; hers left home and never once looked back.

We all have a dark side. Most of us go through life avoiding direct confrontation with that aspect of ourselves, which I call

*"If it'll keep my heart soft, break my heart every day."*

~WARSAN SHIRE

*"The whole purpose of automatic writing is to access guidance from your Soul, especially if you struggle to hear it in daily life."*

~ALETHEIA LUNA

the shadow self. There's a reason why we avoid our shadow self. It takes a great deal of energy.

By acknowledging traits we habitually hide from ourselves—whether it be a sense we are not good enough or have caused harm—or try to rationalize away, we serve our soul by willingly and consciously confronting our own shadow, our darkest self.

### Body Sensations

Sensations in the body, such as tingles, heat, and breath, reflect your psyche's needs. Your body contains many memories and secrets—both "good" and uncomfortable ones—and feelings in the body are there to alert you to a deeper state of your being. It may seem that body pain and pleasure are circumstantial experiences, which doesn't tell us much. That's a limited view of the body and its relationship to the soul. In truth, your body's feelings often reflect your psyche's needs. Awareness about your body is a wake-up call to regain contact with the inner self and reach beyond self-consciousness, toward seamless immersion in the purpose of your life.

Say you're reading a book you love; there is no space between you and the story. When you are focused on it, the world falls away, and you are at one with the experience. That's what you aim for, being "in the zone" and living in a state where your insides match your outsides. You want to be where the story and the reader become one.

When do you last remember having no sense of time? Perhaps you were involved in a story or a conversation. Perhaps you were writing or drawing. Write about what feels timeless to you.

### Community Reflection (Loving Tree)

Sometimes it's hard to see ourselves clearly, so it helps to surround ourselves with people we trust who can remind us of who we really are or help translate and interpret our experiences when we are bogged down and can't see the way.

*"The body is a multilingual being. It speaks through its color and its temperature, the flush of recognition, the glow of love, the ash of pain, the heat of arousal, the coldness of non-conviction. . . It speaks through the leaping of the heart, the falling of the spirits, the pit at the center, and rising hope."*

~CLARISSA PINKOLA ESTÉS

The Himba tribe of southern Africa has a unique method of reminding tribe members of who they are: They sing the person's song back at them.

The Himba tribe is one of the few that counts the birthdate of children not from the day they are born or conceived, but the day the mother decides to have the child. When she decides, she goes off and sits under a tree, by herself, and listens until she can hear the song of the child who wants to come. After she's heard the song of this child, she comes back to the man who will be the child's father and teaches him the song. When they make love to physically conceive the child, they sing the song of the child as a way of inviting him or her into the world.

When she becomes pregnant, the mother teaches that child's song to the midwives and the old women of the village, so that when the child is born, the people who gather around the child can sing his song to welcome him. As the child grows up, other villagers are taught the child's song. If the child falls, or gets hurt, someone picks him up and sings him his song. When the child does something wonderful or passes through the rites of puberty, the people of the village honor the child by singing his song.

One other occasion calls for the child's song to be sung. If a tribe member commits a crime or something that is against the Himba social norms, the villagers call him into the center of the village and the community forms a circle around him. Then they sing his birth song to him.

The Himba view this moment as a correction, not as a punishment, but as love and remembrance of identity. When you recognize your own song, you have no desire or need to do anything that would hurt another person. In marriage, the songs of the man and the woman are sung together. When the Himba tribe member is lying in his bed, ready to die, all the villagers that know his song come and sing his song for the last time.

Do you have a song? What is it? How does it tell us who you are? Does your song change from day to day? How and why? Does your friend have a song? What is it? Have you ever sung each other's song by way of greeting? Try it.

## Stress

Feeling "stressed" is a catch-all term that means nothing except that you cannot express how and what you feel; it's all a wall of anger and exhaustion. Your soul is on lockdown and you feel almost nothing but a free-floating, unsourced anger.

Your physical being is screaming at you and if you don't listen, injury to your body, mind, and soul will result. One of the reasons for Morning Practice is it creates a sense of opening and coming home to yourself which occurs as peace to start your day; it is money in the bank for when stress comes.

If you feel "stressed," what exactly are you feeling? What do you believe to be the underlying reason? Write about it.

What are the things you feel angry or frustrated about? Write them down. Write them down as though no one else will see this list; get them all out on paper.

## Writing and Drawing

Writing and drawing are essential tools for exploring your own soul; you dive down and let what comes come, then rise refreshed, rejuvenated, and renewed. Carl Jung asked his patients to make their own books, drawing, journaling, and scribbling down ideas and random thoughts. He encouraged them to make their own archetypes; one's mother could be The Destroyer or The Rescuer, while one's father may be The Punisher or The Runner. In this way, they told of their soul's passage, or *nekyia*, through the psychic underworld, in a therapeutic practice that neutralized negative thoughts and traumatic memory.

Put it all down as beautifully as you can. It may seem as if you were making the visions banal, but then you need to do that, and you are freed from the power of them . . . "Then when these things are in some precious book, you can go to the book and turn over the pages and for you it will be your church, your cathedral, the silent places of your spirit where you will find renewal. If anyone tells you that it is morbid or neurotic and you listen to

*"Stress is the gift that alerts you to your asleepness. Feelings like anger or sadness exist only to alert you to the fact that you're believing your own stories."*

~BYRON KATIE

them. Then you will lose your soul, for in that book is your soul."
~from *Analysis Notebooks*, quoted in *The Red Book, Liber Novus*, by
C.G. Jung

## Visions During Meditation

Meditating for ten minutes or more is a powerful way to feel what
has been referred to as the mystical experience. One common
mystical experience involves tuning in to visions or insights while
you're meditating. During meditation, an entire scene drops into
your mind, seemingly out of nowhere, or you might hear words
or curious thoughts.

Mystical experiences are so powerful, they have changed
the course of human history. They unleash creative energies and
often provide effortless solutions to some of life's greatest challenges. They are without end. The more you meditate, the more
mystical experiences you have.

A master of meditation says, "Let me sit with it." And they
mean just that. By simply being still and clearing the mind, you
invite a miraculous world in. When you "sit with it," what do you
hear and see?

*"Champions aren't made in the gyms. Champions are made from something they have deep inside them—a desire, a dream, a vision."*

~MUHAMMAD ALI

## Desire

Desires are your soul speaking to you, telling you what it wants.
You may crave intimacy or chocolate cake. Desires in and of
themselves are beyond "good" and "bad"; they just are. Accepting
that you have them is not the same as acting upon them, and only
you know what is "good" or "bad" for your soul. It's your acre of
land, remember?

Do you feel a specific desire or desires? Write about it. What
do you want? List five things you want today and five things you
want this month. Be specific. The more specific your desire, the
more you will be able to be with it in your body.

*"Which we call libido, and whose nature it is to bring forth the useful and the harmful, the good and the bad."*

~C.G. JUNG

## Meditation

*"Meditation does not itself accomplish the tasks of life but provides spaciousness, bringing the great background near, so that whatever we do, rising in the quiet, has force and beauty. In meditation, we take time, sit down, watch, while the silence accumulates–which is how the spirit gathers to a vessel the soul has prepared."*

~JOHN TARRANT

As far as we know, meditation has been practiced for at least 2,500 years. Why? As great a gift as it is to be able to think the way human beings do, thinking alone cannot make a person whole. In truth, thinking often gets in the way of knowing our whole selves. It can interfere with knowing things, in ways that are greater than ourselves. At worst, thinking can feel like sheer torture.

Sometimes we need a break. This is the simplest reason to meditate. But thinking is a natural process. No matter how hard you try, you can't just stop thinking. It can't be willed away any more than you can will away breathing.

We find another way. We learn to watch our thoughts rather than getting ourselves tangled up in them. As someone chooses to develop a practice of sitting quietly, breathing, and watching her own thinking, when she is ready, a change will begin to occur. It may start slowly as her river of thoughts begins to slow. And then it may become clearer, that while she has been watching the mud and the rocks and debris wash by, she has been missing something else in the stream of thoughts, something that can only be seen as the waters still, and it is glittering like gold at the bottom.

Ultimately, meditation is for that: to help us see clearly and come to realize that the gold in the river is You.

Find a quiet place. If you can't find a quiet place, find the quietest place you can. If you have a way to track the time, that will be helpful.

There are two options for sitting.

One is on a chair with your feet flat on the floor.

The other is to get a pillow and find a place on the floor or a bed where you can sit, cross-legged on the pillow.

You will want to sit on the edge of the pillow, which may need folding in half for more height to allow for the slight natural curve at the base of your spine. This is what's called a "straight back." Everyone's body is different, so everyone has different needs for creating the right position to sit.

It takes a little experimenting.

If you're sitting on a chair, you may find that you need to sit forward a bit to get your feet flat on the ground and keep your back straight. When seated either on a chair or the floor, tilt the top of your pelvis forward slightly. This allows you to ground down through the front of the sitz bones.

If you're sitting cross-legged on a blanket, you might need to put some extra cushioning like a sweatshirt or towel under each knee. Sitting cross-legged, you may think of your knees and pelvis creating a triangular base above which the spine can balance. Find out for yourself what gives you the greatest stability and ease, as a position.

So now you're sitting.

You sit down all the time; what's the difference with this?

To start with, instead of sitting down, you might try sitting up. And instead of making a command of yourself, try making a request.

Can I grow taller inside myself? What does that feel like?

Can I draw air into my body more easily when I sit up this way? Or that?

Does my spine feel more supportive when it's in alignment with my head and my hips?

These are some questions you might want to ask yourself. You're looking for what's really happening with your body, not what you think should be happening. And if you can't maintain the sitting-up posture for long, don't worry about it. Move to a more comfortable position and come back to sitting more upright when you're ready.

Once you're sitting, you probably want to close your eyes, so you won't be distracted by what's outside you. Now turn your attention to your breathing. You don't have to do anything about it, just watch what it's doing. Is it fast? Slow? Ragged? Smooth? Can you watch your breath without trying to change it in any way? It may change itself but see if you can watch for that to happen. Or not.

This is the soft, wild animal of yourself you're watching, and she's doing what she does all the time quite well, without your attention. But pay attention now. Keep watching your breaths.

Thinking often stands in the way of quieting the mind, criticizing, or judging how and what you're doing. And it's okay. Thinking is okay. But in this practice, thinking is not the boss.

To keep the thinking part of yourself occupied, you might want to try counting your breaths, from one to ten. That's all. You reach ten and start over at one. Sometimes this is enough to satisfy your thinking mind. Sometimes you'll find it wanders off somewhere else and you lose track of the breaths you were counting. That's fine. Just start over at one. You can always go back to one. All you want to do is to keep sitting.

Try to sit for ten minutes at first. This is a good place to begin meditating.

You may find it relaxing. You may find it dull as dirt. No matter what you find it now, just know that it will change. Try to remember that thinking itself doesn't want to be quieted. Thinking will want to get back to its usual chatter and position of calling all the shots. It really doesn't always know what's good for it. But if you make a firm decision to keep sitting, no matter what your thoughts seem to say, you may find at some point that you've learned to grow taller and quieter inside. And just that is a relief.

Close your eyes. Watch your breath.

Within ten minutes, you may begin to get the sense that your mind is like a snow globe, and as you sit, it will be like watching the snow settle to the floor.

When the ten minutes becomes easier, you can increase your sitting to fifteen minutes. Notice the difference in your mind and body doing that. When that becomes comfortable, try twenty minutes. Don't skip straight to fifteen or twenty minutes to start. Take your time. You want to notice the differences along the way.

If you make a firm decision to keep sitting no matter what your thoughts seem to say, you may find at some point that you've learned to grow taller and quieter inside. Just that is a relief.

There is more to this, but this is where it begins.

The gold is inside; it's right *here*, in you.

*"Recall my words to you here and now and reflect on them when you feel that old habit or that pang of insecurity that's nagging in the back of your mind saying, 'You know they're right, you are not good enough, you are not pretty enough.' All you've got to do is look in your heart of hearts, and feel how your heart beats; it beats to your soul's drum. It's not a skin color, it's not a race that has it beating so fiercely, it's your essence."*

~Willie, Texas Dept. of Criminal Justice, Ferguson Unit

# THE HIDDEN MASTER

## Basic Goodness

The mind is a powerful warden. The body, our soul, our refuge and salvation, can often seem difficult to enter. Some have left themselves so long ago, they forgot that home is within.

Looking for your own self-worth from the outside world, energy, and talents is aimed at continuing to elicit someone, or something, to say, "Yes, you are good." We live in a state of sinking, hopping from inflated life raft to life raft as people affirm our value. Perhaps you have grown accustomed to hanging on to these rafts, to hearing the air slowly escape and the dark water slowly pulling you down. This is what we consider hell: living locked out of ourselves.

This pattern continues. If it is not a good deed, it is the right job. You will be happy when you find the right job. It may be the perfect partner, the perfect family. Everything, anything, but you.

When you've lost track of your innate goodness, everything you experience gets measured against, "Does this make me good or make me bad?" This is why we grasp at success and drown in failure. We strive for that brief "pleasing" and "winning" feeling, at the cost of inner peace and a clean conscience. Who are we pleasing? What do we win?

In the hardest of times, how do we remember that what is inside of us is made of Good? Everywhere we look we are reminded of hurt, and the reminder of hurt instills a sense of shame. The shame and hurt pierce through "I did something wrong," and we can begin to believe "I am something wrong."

Facing what seem like insurmountable challenges, you may have already given up the idea of your life having value or ever being able to enjoy it. You might even feel you live beyond redemption; the cause of "you" is lost.

Start with the challenging idea that you are perfect and were perfectly created for love. This lesson flows through every other lesson in the soulmaker's progress. You may feel uncomfortable at first because of other programming you've received. Let's melt through that and get to love.

*"It's not that we have little time, but more that we waste a good deal of it."*

~SENECA

None of us were born with self-hatred. Recount a time you felt valued. It probably involved other people. It probably involved feeling in some way connected to something greater than yourself—a family, a community of friends, a school, coworkers, a sense of purpose. The feeling of self-worth was tied to your sense of being connected and belonging to something other than yourself. At once you felt both fulfilled personally and that you had a place. This is not an idea or something you gain. It's a human experience to which we all have a claim.

There is a place. Beyond this place, there is a field. In that field, right and wrong do not exist. This is where we ask you to meet us. We discover an indescribable beauty when we break through the belief that we must earn our way. There is such a thing as real wealth, and that is wealth of the soul. It is a wealth that says you do not live paycheck to paycheck of your last good deed, or rely on the last person who smiled at you and acknowledged you as a human. This wealth is something you were endowed with when you came onto this earth. It is not a wealth you earn; it is a wealth you remember. We are here to help walk you home to this memory.

This is all to say, value is not a man-made concept. An innocent place lives inside you and it never changes, no matter what; it's a quality that no one can take away, not even you. Receiving and giving love exists in every heart beating beneath every ribcage; there's nothing anyone can do or say to change that.

After we accept our basic goodness, we will still feel pain. Life continues to go on, on life's terms. But we approach the pain differently. We shift away from running from it and come to see it as the sign that more awakening is near. The sting doesn't lessen, but the experience of the sting changes with this new sense of purpose. Our experience of pain becomes a part of our path toward our genius, our higher purpose.

Whatever your injuries may be, this course is about shifting your mind, so you begin to see problems and difficult emotions in your life as opportunities to deepen your experience of your life, to carve out more of the emotional scar tissue. Stop performing

*"We already have everything we need."*

~PEMA CHÖDRÖN.

for others and work on building a relationship with yourself and your Higher Power, your Creator, your God.

## God as You Understand God

You decide what God is for you. You decide what word you use too: God, Spirit, Higher Power, Universe, Divine Order, Great Mystery, Creator, Home. No matter what you want to call it, there is an energy that runs through all things, from you to your mother and your child and great-grandparents and back into your community, then back up to that Higher Power or Home, looping around again and again, endlessly moving through everything. Though this course is secular, we will use the term God, for simplicity. You get to define God for yourself, just as you get to write your story of your own life.

Soulmaking requires believing that something greater than ourselves decides our worth and our value; that you and I are here because we're supposed to be here. In soulmaking, the moment you decide you don't have worth or do have worth is a Godless moment; you do not have the power to make that call. God decides, and God believes in you.

It's not about solving the problems that the world, or your mind, presents. That's just another version of "doing" better, twisting in knots, and jumping to achieve the approval of others. Our sense of self-worth is about shifting our consciousness entirely, to one rooted in our basic goodness. Then you will offer yourself to the situations you experience instead of needing to "get" something from them.

*"The altar, as in prehistory, is anywhere you kneel."*

~CAMILLE PAGLIA

Once a person touches this freedom and flexibility in their mind, nothing else will do. There's an old saying that goes: "Once you've had one taste of the divine, nothing else will do, and you will do anything to get it." You've exited the enslavement of proving yourself to others. You can inhale deep into your belly—long, slow breaths. You can savor air, you can savor your body nourishing from your breath. The simple becomes profound.

We believe that, for reasons only God understands, our

traumas, setbacks, and difficulties are all a part of our path as a human being. We are here to teach you how to get "in" to your life, how to get rooted so deeply into the reality of your present experience that you are able to sink below or rise above the daily "fight" of life, and tap into a new way of living, centered in the heart. In this new way, your focus remains on finding the presence of love everywhere. This is what God intends for all of us.

The first step is to choose to suspend disbelief, in the name of discovering and experiencing this new way. The choice is to suspend fighting your current circumstances to settle into your present life, and yourself; to find out why you are here. By looking within yourself, you will always see only good, because that's what's there.

*"The shamans say that being a medicine man begins by falling into the power of the demons; The one who pulls out of the dark place becomes the medicine man, and the one who stays in it is the sick person."*

~JOAN HALIFAX

# Integration Exercises

Each day of this first week's lesson, after you've finished your Morning Practice, answer a question below in writing. Take as much time and space as you desire.

*Beliefs*

■ What's something of value I offer to the people around me?

■ Who do I love?

■ Who loves me?

■ Who do I trust? Why do I trust them?

■ What is the meaning of my life?

- What do I offer to myself?

*Seeking Approval from Others*

- What limiting beliefs remain in me that say I am bad or weak?

- In what ways do I look to people outside of myself for approval, rather than having courage to offer myself?

- When have I allowed others to speak negatively about me and not stood up?

- Where did I accommodate cultural norms and pretend that I could or would change?

- Where did I bow to public opinion and betray the deeper meaning of my life?

- Where have I used my skills for personal gain and not given back?

*"I don't really like to call any feelings or states solely 'good' or 'bad.' To me, they are just like greed, delusion, jealousy, etc. I can't perceive them as 'good,' but they are opportunities to re-channel energy into something productive. This is what I'm trying to do with myself!"*

~Diana Lovejoy,
Central California Women's Facility

# GET BACK TO WHERE YOU ONCE BELONGED

Learn to convert pain's poison into the antidote: strength. By staying with uncomfortable or hurtful feelings, you burn out the negative energy, the charge. We'll show you how to do it so that you may let go of what does not serve you.

## Defining the Challenge

Most people, whether in prison or on the outside, live inside a "cell." The cell may not be made of metal, but they have locked up their thoughts and emotions and very lives, living as the poet said, "in quiet desperation."

Take the woman with the perfect house, the perfect husband, and the perfect kids. She smiles as she walks through the grocery store, smiles as she passes her neighbor's home. She gets home, and she is exhausted. She woke up not knowing if she could make it through the day smiling, but she did. She doesn't know if she can smile tomorrow. Each day gets harder. Sometimes she notices how hard it is; other times, she's forgotten. Her husband, growing distant, wants to reach her, but can't. He doesn't know how. He makes more money to remodel their house; he spends more time with the kids. She can't shake the unhappiness, the haunted feeling there is another life she was meant to live.

We need to understand the mechanics of what we call suffering. Suffering exists regardless of your circumstances. The physical place doesn't matter. Suffering is most characterized by the belief, "If I get X, then I will be happy." It is the lack of presence in the world. More specifically, it is the refusal to accept life in the present, until your demands are met. "I will be happy when I get out. I will be happy when my husband comes back. I will be happy when my health improves." This is suffering.

People go to great lengths to avoid confronting this suffering, hiding from pain and feelings. At worst, they go dead inside, refusing to experience the dynamism and pleasure of being human.

*"What is required of us is that we love the difficult and learn to deal with it. In the difficult are the friendly forces, the hands that work on us. Right in the difficult we must have our joys, our happiness, our dreams: there against the depth of this background, they stand out, there for the first time we see how beautiful they are."*

~RAINER MARIA RILKE

*"When another person makes you suffer, it is because he suffers deeply within himself, and his suffering is spilling over. He does not need punishment; he needs help. That's the message he is sending."*

~THICH NHAT HANH

The only way to experience unconditional freedom—and we mean unconditional—is to look into the depth of your emotions and voices of your soul and feel them. Acceptance is what sets us all free.

Every human being experiences pain. It could be physical pain from accidents, injuries, or abuse. Emotional pain from moments of being hurt or feeling rejected, abandoned, or betrayed. Perhaps a sense of emotional guilt and shame snakes through you—dark, persistent feelings that you failed at life or let people down.

Few have the tools to deal with pain. You can act out against it, reject it and live in exhausting denial, avoid and numb it with drugs or alcohol or junk food or, worst of all, try to fix it, which is definitely above your pay grade in life. Only God "fixes" the world; you must stay in your body, closer to home.

This pain is moving as a ghost might move through your own life. At its worst, things feel empty, pointless, lacking; you cannot find meaning. You feel resigned to live this way with no hope of enjoyment, just an endless sense of going through the motions.

In Far East cultures such as those of China, Vietnam, and India, a Hungry Ghost is depicted as a spirit with a bloated stomach and a throat so narrow that eating is incredibly painful, even impossible. This represents a hunger that cannot be fed: the lingering sensation of a tangible, insatiable hunger. The Ghost can never be gratified by any amount of consumption. Think of the Ghost as the poor kid who could never be rich enough as an adult; a first-generation American who never feels "American" enough; or an ex-lover wandering the world looking to recreate an old childhood dynamic, never able to meet someone as they are. Their stomachs will never fill.

People spend their entire lives hiding from pain. They find others who also hide; they go on hiding from pain together. False personas meet false personas, but no real intimacy is ever created. They form common bonds as victims to other people or institutions. Think of the group of men who all grumble about their jobs, sharing with certainty their displeasure, but never improving their lives individually. They live with chronic complaints.

Or instead they bond around a common enemy, creating connection through complaint and counteraggression. Or perhaps they are the "nice" ones, the ones there for support, shaking their heads at the carelessness of others. The group of nice ones may feel commonality, but no one ever feels truly reached. No person gets to be truly seen and known. Whole lives, families, and organizations are built in this way, people speaking across desks and tables for years, never really seeing or knowing each other.

Harvesting is a term used for gathering food, from plants to fish and meat. You harvest vegetables from plants or shoot a deer to harvest its meat. In a larger sense, you can gather anything, but if you cannot harvest your own pain, you will be buried by it. It will grow to define you. Pain and discomfort give you impulse to act, but taking action distracts you from the real work of identifying and knowing the pain enough that it will reveal its secrets to you. Essentially, our "doing," our endless busy-ness, chatter, and diversions, keep us from our "being"—our consciousness. That is the cause of our suffering.

## Victim Consciousness

Our thoughts determine the quality of our life experience. Some of our thoughts have been with us since the beginning; many were inherited from our family members. These "core" beliefs could easily be called our unquestioned assumptions. They are unquestioned, yet we let them define us and our world. We let these beliefs create our story about who we are and what we can expect from the world.

Victimhood snakes through the consciousness of many, squeezing and squeezing the life out of them; victimhood feels more like the snake than anything Adam and Eve encountered. Its shape might surprise you. The head of this snake is fear, the fear you will not survive, either physically or mentally. The good news,

*"Those who do not move, do not notice their chains."*
~ROSA LUXEMBURG

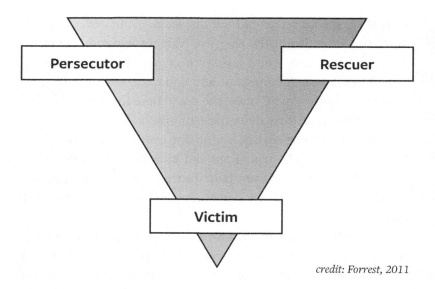

*credit: Forrest, 2011*

and there is a little, is that being a victim implies that within you is a *victor*.

Being a victim also means you feel entitled: *I worked hard and that is my promotion. I was a great girlfriend and he left me. I do everything for my kids, and they don't care one bit.*

You feel entitled to the job, the man, and the love of your family, and as soon as you embrace your role in the victimhood (the weight of your expectations set up the Victim Triangle) you begin to release yourself and move on.

As a victim, you can simmer with anger and plot revenge; but remember, there is no villain without you: the victim.

The Victim Triangle is where the unhappy story of victim consciousness plays out. Adapted from Dr. Stephen Karpman's Drama Triangle, the Victim Triangle, as presented by Lynne Forrest, explains how our various defense strategies—victim, persecutor, and rescuer—interact (Forrest, 2011). We learn that we perpetuate our unhappy story when we believe our thoughts, and in so doing, we go from point to point on the Victim Triangle.

Each position has its own way of seeing and reacting to the world. To help better understand the three roles, consider these stories from the perspective of rescuer, persecutor, and victim.

## Rescuer

Sally's mother was physically disabled and addicted to prescription drugs. From Sally's earliest memory, she reported feeling ultimately responsible for her mother. Instead of getting appropriate care from a parent who was concerned for her well-being, she became the "little parent" of a mother who played the part of a helpless child.

This childhood scenario set Sally up with a "life script" that predisposed her toward becoming a rescuer. Caretaking of others became her primary way of relating to other human beings.

Rescuers like Sally have an unconscious core belief that might go something like this: *My needs are not important. I am only valued for what I can do for others.* Of course, believing these ideas requires her to have someone in her life who she can rescue: a victim. How else would someone like Sally feel valuable and worthwhile?

Sally would never admit to being a victim because, in her mind, she is the one who must have the answers. Nonetheless, she does rotate through the victim position on the triangle on a regular basis. A rescuer in the victim role becomes a martyr, complaining loudly, "After all I've done for you, this is the thanks I get?" (Forrest, 2011).

## Persecutor

Bob is a doctor who often justified hurting others. Attack was his primary way of dealing with inconvenience, frustration, or pain. Once, for instance, he mentioned running into a patient on the golf course. "Can you believe that patient had the nerve to ask me to treat his bad knee right then and there on my only day off?" Bob handled it by taking his patient to his office and giving him "a steroid shot he'll never forget."

In other words, Bob rescued his inconsiderate patient, but in a way that "punished" him for daring to be so bold. To Bob, his action seemed rational, even justified. His patient had infringed on his free time; therefore he deserved the rough treatment. This is a prime example of persecutor thinking. Bob didn't realize that he could have just said no to his patient's request for treatment. He did not have to feel victimized by or need to rescue his patient. Setting boundaries never occurred as an option to Bob. In his mind, he had been treated unjustly and therefore he had the right, even the obligation, to get even (Forrest, 2011).

## Victim

Janette sees herself as consistently unable to handle life. She sees simple chores (like doing laundry, cleaning the bathroom, and preparing meals) as overwhelming tasks. Constantly complaining of exhaustion, Janette says to her partner, "You're the only one who can help me." She feels bad about herself and her inner dialogue is just plain mean. She thinks her own harsh critical voice might be right about how incapable and incompetent she is.

You can enter the Victim Triangle from any point, but the movement and resolution you seek will never come as you drain your energy on this merry-go-round. Get out of it. Now.

## The Hardest Work Is to Stay with Yourself

Why do we hop onto the Victim Triangle? Because it is uncomfortable to sit in the sensation of our pain. We want to do something, react wildly, and expel it from our bodies. It's fundamentally about not taking responsibility—not in the way society chastises us for not taking responsibility, throwing out meaningless phrases such as "You're lazy," or "You're lying." Remember, responsibility is not about what you do or don't do. It is about not taking responsibility for remembering your "beingness."

The temptation that follows this knee-jerk reaction in your insides, this desire to chatter, busy yourself, and bolt from the challenge, is never about shiny objects outside of ourselves. These restless feelings are about running from our own insides, and any place is more comfortable than there.

These fierce, mindless reactions undermine our faith. We try to take matters into our own hands. We worry, *If I surrender, who will defend me?* We get locked out of wisdom and locked into the delusion that the relief lies in winning, no matter what the "win" is. But the true work our souls are calling for is the work to stay rooted in our hearts, in the face of the temptation to flip out and lose ourselves. Can I love it here? Bringing your pain to the center of your heart is bringing your pain to God.

The avoidance patterns are endless. From victimhood, to perpetration, to denial, to compensation through achievement, drugs, and food, the list of addictions goes on. All of these methods end in the same result: continually diminishing returns, because the more you use them, the less they work. The more you use anger to cover up fear, the angrier you get. The more you use happiness to cover up pain, the happier you must pretend to be.

## The Antidote Is Made from the Venom

The very thing that there is so much of—pain—turns out to be the exact ingredient needed to transform your mind and your interior world from an unpredictable, tumultuous roller coaster into something more like your own inner temple.

Pain is a lot like soil. Soil is made up of dirt and nutrients that decay; everything in life that has died or been released to the ground somehow carries the nutrients that grow all plants, flowers, vegetables, and fruits. Everything that life is. Pain is to creativity as soil is to plants. Pain is the ground where creativity grows.

Say an addict gets sober and helps others get sober. She relates with their very dark descent and terrible experiences, helping other addicts see it's possible to have a new life. The pain, and the clear-eyed examination of it, resets and regenerates them all; their lives have meaning. Addiction has thus become a pathway into the soul; its pain and passion are redirected toward strength, healing, and higher purpose.

*"I imagine one of the reasons people cling to their hates so stubbornly is because they sense, once hate is gone, they will be forced to deal with pain."*
~JAMES BALDWIN

*"One word frees us of all the weight and pain of life: That word is love."*

~SOPHOCLES

When we have a solid footing of freedom within, it doesn't matter if we are being treated unfairly. Is life really a mistake? Is this situation really too much? In what way? We can spend a life avoiding pain and at the end of it, look back and find we have the same resentments we always did. Pain ran our life and now that life is ending.

We spend our lives avoiding the discomfort of pain, but facing it turns out to be the medicine that eases the discomfort. The antidote is made from the venom. Just look at Alcoholics Anonymous: When someone stands and says, "My name is X, and I am an alcoholic," the room surges with power. The Catholic sacrament of confession works on the same principle. The truth of simply stating a secret does in fact create a space, a freedom, inside.

All that matters is, can you find peace within? Are you willing to do whatever it takes to achieve that peace? God sends us places and asks us to do the work.

You happen to have received one of God's hardest assignments. But God reserves His hardest assignments for His toughest soldiers.

## Integration Exercises

Questions to consider in your daily Letter to Your Soul practice:

- Where did I allow my victim archetype to take me hostage in a situation?

- What were the results?

- Have I done the work to truly fortify my backbone?

- Where can I claim responsibility in my life?

- What secrets do I need to get on paper today?

*"Here's the bad news: You can't get 'over' a feeling . . .*
*Here's the good news: You do not heal feelings,*
*you see, they heal you."*

~JEFF FOSTER, FROM "LET A FEELING CRACK YOU OPEN"

*"Pain comes with the human experience and avoiding it cheats us out of great lessons. Show me someone who has never experienced hardship or heartache. That person can't fathom depth. We come to realize how easy it is to not be caught up in the pain, to recognize it, to understand it, but not to attach to it."*

~Donald Dillbeck, Union Correctional Institution, Florida

# EVERY VOICE INSIDE IS TRYING TO HELP YOU

This lesson is more pain conversion work, as you learn to use alchemy to transmute difficult experiences into positive ones. In this way, you come to see that even what you perceive as "bad" is good.

## How to Harvest Pain

Everything we experience carries a secret for us, and it is our work in this world to find out what that secret is. Until we do, this experience will recur, over and over, until we can grow to receive it. Some of these experiences are positive. We will meet someone who reminds us of a loving friend we were never able to be good to in return, and our second encounter grants us the opportunity to mend where we fell short the first time. In other cases, it's a negative experience. A loved one dies, followed shortly after by another. We are turned down on the spot from two job interviews, two days in a row.

These experiences carry with them their own emotional heaviness. For example, they incite in us joy, disgust, shame, or grief. Each experience is its own initiation, its own entry point into liminality. That is a transition point for our soul. Our soul will attempt again and again to reconcile us with it. It is our bell, ringing over and over to bring us home to ourselves.

If God (however we understand God) intends for us to be naturally joyous and free, then it holds true that we can be joyous and free anywhere. Each experience is our opportunity to confront all the limitations of our mind, which would otherwise have us not feel joy and freedom. This process is like a polishing stone, slowly rubbing out the kinks to reveal our natural brightness.

At all times the soul's calling is to receive. The soul does not choose what is good or bad. It does not say, "I will feel this, but not that." Or "I will let you affect me, but I will not let you affect

*"Knowing your own darkness is the best method for dealing with the darknesses of other people."*

~C. G. JUNG

me." Just as our souls are durable, remaining alive and thriving wherever we are, they are also entirely permeable. These qualities come with a soul. The more we let down our guard, the more we begin to see how deeply sensitive we are to everyone and everything. Where the spirit says that this sensitivity is weakness, and our job is to become untouchable, the soul says that our sensitivity is our strength and our window into the interconnected reality of nature.

The soul simply cannot fake it. You will experience this everywhere. You will walk into a room and have an intuition of how your friends are feeling. You will sit down to eat, and immediately sense the tempo of the conversation already happening. Perhaps someone is emotional, and the people are heavy and grave. Perhaps it is a more boisterous day; jokes are being told, and laughter is spilling off the table. This is your antennae, taking in information, informing you of your environment, and in this process you are changed. You are sensitized and sensitive, a highly useful state as you receive information.

Our pain carries our greatest secrets. The greater the pain, the greater the secret.

*"It's how you see it. What really for me was a change in point was looking for the good that could come out of my bad situation. I purposely looked for it, and I molded that thing until I could see it—pit bull focus—and now, you know what, I'm living it."*

~JAMILA DAVIS, AMERICAN AUTHOR, ACTIVIST, AND FORMER FEDERAL PRISONER #59253-053

## Soulmaker's Essential

### *Mastering Alchemy*

An alchemist's job is to turn one material into another. We've all heard of the example, "turning lemons into lemonade." The other one is, "turning lead into gold." The alchemist doesn't avoid lemons, nor does he complain about having too much lead. The alchemist relies on the undesirable, often-dismissed materials, because this is his base material for creating gold.

Base materials are what do life's work. We too can stop avoiding pain and actively seek it. When it's present, we can feel it and reorient ourselves to sink further into a relationship with it, because we know the pain was brought to us to be converted to love. Just as developing muscle and strength in the body, pain is the indicator of progress. Feeling pain is knowing there is more humility to be gained. Pain is an indicator that more of our made-up stories and false beliefs need to be stripped away for a greater connection with God. It's said God will never give you more than you can handle.

By harvesting pain, you'll experience a fundamental shift in your life, where you no longer run from uncomfortable emotions or situations. You grow the capacity to let go and relax in a world addicted to achievement, both material and spiritual. You allow yourself to feel rather than act out or have knee-jerk reactions that further your—and other's—pain.

This purpose is the great reward of letting everything enter your heart. This is what we consider true power. You are no longer enslaved to the prejudices and preferences of your mind, which force you to cast blame, deny, and run from the realities of your life. Now you turn and face pain with the intention of letting it in, so that your soul can mold and shape it. Like every master, you'll learn to convert pain to art.

We could call it healing, except we feel healing is too limited a goal. This process of alchemy is the sole purpose of our lives and the fullest expression of our power. Everything we do is in service to this one, single process repeated over and over for the rest of our lives. We face what is in front of us, whether it be a backlog of emotion in our hearts or the accumulation of the injustice we face every day. Instead of fighting it, making it wrong, or denying it, we admit it. We let it in, and let it change us.

How we get where we're going determines what we get when we arrive. Like building a house, if you take care and use quality materials, the chances are better it will weather storms. If you take shortcuts or the foundation is shoddy, it's likely you will pay for it in the end, with interest. This house—your house—is your soul rearranging itself and reaching out beyond useless ideas such as "good" and "bad."

## An Alchemist's Greatest Tool

The answer to every prayer is approval; you are supposed to be here. Approval is synonymous with freedom; approval is not giving in. "Accepting" life as it happens is the capacity to understand that this moment is right because you are in it, this moment is happening. You were destined to meet this moment, and you couldn't stop it if you tried. This moment is right; there is a natural intelligence at work. When you accept the moment, the intelligence goes to work for you. It is why we pray before we encounter difficulty: "God help me." This prayer can help you shoulder and face challenges you otherwise could not.

*"Our feelings are our most genuine paths to knowledge."*

~AUDRE LORDE

We do not pray for the right circumstances to enter our lives; we pray for the power to face the circumstances we are in now. When Jamila Davis found herself facing twelve years in prison for engaging in real estate fraud while working at Lehman Brothers, acceptance was the key to her freedom. She could not be endlessly bitter about the fact that she had landed in jail for doing the same thing many others got away with doing. Her high-flying career, brokering real estate deals for hip-hop artists and other celebrities, was over. In facing her new reality, she became a stronger and more powerful person than she ever was making deals in designer clothes in New York. Jamila had the power of approval, and it launched her on a long arc of community-building and service. The "lead" of prison turned into the "gold" of a new, deeply meaningful life.

Approval is neutral. You are simply acknowledging what is, and that you are willing to be with it, because you know that being with something (without trying to change it) is how you harvest the benefit it is trying to offer you. Whatever life throws your way—pain, hurt, betrayal, regret, remorse—you can acknowledge it while staying firmly seated inside the house of your value.

Understand: Approval is not endorsement. Approval is not saying difficult experiences are deserved or another person's poor behavior is acceptable. It's easy to confuse approval with endorsement, which is why people often disapprove of things. We can be so doggedly determined that something is wrong, we trick ourselves into refusing to see it is happening. But of course, this is a strategy of a consciousness that remains stubbornly rooted in acknowledging only the reality we want to see. The more mature mind sees that you can have approval for something without saying it's okay that it happened, and without liking it. You can approve of it, while not endorsing it. This isn't simply a choice of words; this is a choice that determines the story of your life. When you refuse to acknowledge something has happened, it rules you. When you acknowledge what has happened, you can then choose how you want to be with it.

Consider the story of a Black author who interviewed the leader of the Ku Klux Klan (KKK) to better understand his views. They continued correspondence and eventually a friendship grew. The Black man even attended KKK rallies led by the leader. They would embrace, even call each other friends for more than ten years, though all the while the KKK leader stood by his position that Black people are inferior.

> *"The events of the world do not form an orderly queue, like the English. They crowd around chaotically, like Italians."*
>
> ~CARLO ROVELLI,
> THE ORDER OF TIME

Fifteen years into their friendship, the KKK leader came to his own natural conclusion: He'd been wrong. He denounced his position, retired his KKK robe, and began talking to others about the limitations of racism. Fifteen members of his KKK chapter left with him.

The punishment model would have shamed the KKK leader as a racist, forbade him from speaking his viewpoints, and forced him underground. However, the ancestry of racism would not be converted to love. It would have continued on, more underground, for the next generation. But in this case, through the heart, there was a genuine healing, and everyone was better off for the experience. No one was cast out, ostracized, or shamed, and future generations of those families will understand more about their experience.

What we hope you learn is a way to enact change by doing something other than being victimized or attacking, dominating, or threatening a perpetrator into submission. That simply results in the same old loop: victim to perpetrator and back again. We hope you'll learn a deeper reconciliation with anyone or anything that has you locked out of your heart. By making friends with this pain, in this case racism, you begin to change the racist's mind. You begin their healing and, most importantly, yours.

*"If you bring forth what is within you, what you bring forth will save you. If you do not bring forth what is within you, what you do not bring forth will destroy you."*

~GOSPEL OF THOMAS

## Integration Exercises

- What was the most painful experience you had as a child?

- Did something good come from that pain?

- What was the most painful experience you ever had as an adult?

- Did something good come from that pain?

- Do these experiences have any commonalities? What are they?

- What is the pain that seems unbearable? Not able to alchemize?

- What would it look like to write out how this pain could benefit others around you?

*"Until recently, I didn't express how I felt but I learned that the more I open up, the more I heal. When we forgive someone, there is a healthy balance of boundaries and internal peace as we grow and heal."*

~Daniell, Central California Women's Facility

# YOU WERE CHOSEN FOR FORGIVENESS

## LESSON 4

Forgiveness is essential for a whole human life. It can come like a bolt from heaven or take decades of difficult work. Learning to forgive is an imperative for external as well as internal peace.

## "The Choice"

In Iran, Samereh Alinejad suffered a mother's worst fear: Her teenage son was stabbed to death by his friend, Balal, when the boys were just eighteen. From that day forward, rage and thoughts of revenge consumed her; little else was on her mind. Balal was caught, tried, and sentenced to death. That country's penal code gives the victim's family a final say in capital punishment, and Samereh awaited the day she could take this man's life, just as he had taken her son's. She longed for it in fact.

In the months leading up to the execution, Samereh's dead son came to her in dreams, asking her to spare his friend Balal. The dreams did nothing to soften her desire to see him dead. In the last dream before the scheduled hanging, Samereh dreamed her son would not speak to her. She did not waver. "An eye for an eye" is a fundamental part of Islamic justice, or "sharia law."

On the day of the execution, Samereh's family dressed carefully and went to the prison. Balal's family did as well. As Balal was brought out to the construction crane that would lift him up by the neck until he died, something happened to Samereh. In a flash of "extreme genius," she forgave him. Samereh had never given any indication she would or even could do so. Yet as the noose went around Balal's neck, perhaps she saw in his face the face of her son, a frightened young man doing the best he could in the face of chaos and violence. Perhaps a question ran through her mind, a terrible, terrible question. If she agreed to kill this

*"The weak can never forgive. Forgiveness is the attribute of the strong."*

~MAHATMA GANDHI

*"We must develop and maintain the capacity to forgive. He who is devoid of the power to forgive is devoid of the power to love. There is some good in the worst of us and some evil in the best of us."*

~MARTIN LUTHER KING, JR.

---

*Soulmaker definition: No matter where we go, from ashes to dust, that is God. We experience power as not the power to resist life, but the power to be intimate with it.*

man, what did that make her? Her extreme genius rose in this extreme situation in the most powerful way possible. She intuitively knew circles of violence and hatred don't stop until one side or the other steps up and forgives.

As Balal was taken down from the scaffold, his mother reached through the fence to embrace Samereh, in an emotional moment that transcended time and space. Samereh had stepped into Rumi's field, beyond "rightdoing" or "wrongdoing," and was bathed in the sunlight of motherly love. A photograph of Samereh and Balal's mother went around the world, offering hope to millions.

Samereh forgave herself that day too. She was free of her own hatred and thoughts of violence against this young man who had killed her son. She cast aside her own victimhood. Those thoughts disappeared in that moment of forgiveness. Samereh electrified the world, becoming a hero and symbol of the transformative nature of forgiveness. All her beliefs and pretensions about justifiable punishment fell away when she refused to murder another soul, refused to take another child from another mother. She would not spend life searching for revenge; she chose love instead.

## Your Calling Begins with Forgiveness

No one in power has ever been truly moved by coercion, shame, or force, but rather they are moved naturally. People may change their actions based on being attacked, but real, lasting change of the heart only occurs when their best efforts have been dignified, even when those best efforts fall short. Someone has to offer this acknowledgment first and model a new way. Your initiation into a world of profound inner peace is to become this person.

Your biggest challenge may be self-pity. The lure of this voice is strong, and it will only be reinforced by those around you who dare not make this potentially dangerous journey of forgiveness. If you choose to indulge in it, you fight your calling. You can do everything in your power to get out as fast as you can, or you can collapse in despair. You can live in denial. But you were granted free will after all. If you deny and fight, you won't do what this initiation is here to do: free your soul and in the process, free the souls of others, just like Samereh did.

## What Is Forgiveness?

Forgiveness is as simple as being willing to see the other person, or yourself, as human. We all make mistakes; we are meant to as a way of learning. Forgiveness is connecting to someone's deeper, innocent motivations for acting a certain way. It is opening to understand that everyone is doing the best they can with the (often faulty) maps they were using. It is seeing that systems and institutions are made up of people who are all doing the best they can with their maps as well. It is not condoning terrible behavior or saying terrible harm is okay. It is connecting to the humanity of someone who caused harm, including you, and seeing, touching their innocence underneath it all.

*"Forgiveness does not mean ignoring what has been done or putting a false label on an evil act. It means, rather, that the evil act no longer remains as a barrier to the relationship. Forgiveness is a catalyst creating the atmosphere necessary for a fresh start and a new beginning."*

~MARTIN LUTHER KING, JR.

## What Happens When You Forgive?

You'll notice people start to respond to you differently when you forgive. All of us, including you, are looking for warm, loving eyes to look back at us. God is as well, and quite creatively. Your warm gaze happens at a family picnic and inside a prison; that light is inside you.

Forgiveness changes everyone, beginning with you. Releasing the venom of hatred or resentment from your heart fundamentally changes your capacity. What you previously forbade admission, you now have allowed in. You have followed the calling of your soul, which is to drop the gavel of right and wrong, and instead to receive, and to love.

There is no way to resent someone or a group of people as nasty or cruel without seeing some part of that in you. Forgiveness grants mercy to the humanity of that other person or group of people, and in doing so grants mercy to yourself. You can now

*"To forgive is to set a prisoner free and discover that the prisoner was you."*

~LEWIS B. SMEDES

forgive yourself too. There is no part of you, however deplorable, you ever have to dismiss again.

There is nothing the world needs more than people who rise to this challenge, who find the capability within themselves to answer this sacred call. It can seem like nothing you do from prison could have an impact, but it can, and it does. When someone rises to forgive society, their enemies, their friends, the system, or themselves, they become a person who has freed themselves, regardless of all external conditions. A person like that has untold power, an immense positive impact on whoever they come into contact with. The energy ripples outward in ways you will never see.

## Integration Exercises

- What does forgiveness mean to me?

- Who do I refuse to forgive? Why?

- Who do I benefit by not forgiving?

- Take a moment to write out what it would be like to forgive one person you have deemed unforgivable in your life.

- Without determining you will do it, what does it look like? And what would be required of you?

*"Being here, I have a lot of built-up anger and resentment inside. But I learned long ago that if I was mad at the world all day and the people who put me here, that my time here would be much harder. So, I try to be positive and have an optimistic attitude, but within there is still anger, hurt, and resentment. I am depressed and feel so alone. Even though I try to hide it and put on a facade, it's still there. I would love to learn how to free and release it so I can free and release myself."*

~Leo Kaczmar, Union Correctional Institution, Florida

# AS ABOVE, SO BELOW

# LESSON 5

## Working with the Daimonic

**One of the essential aspects of being alive is learning to deal with any darkness inside yourself—anger, rage, hurt, terror—and harnessing it to create and build.**

There is no greater service on the planet than courageously communicating to the world, by action, as well as word, that one can exist being fully who they are; and beyond that, there is another in the world who is big enough in themselves to welcome who they are. In this way, a soulmaker acknowledges a soulmaker, and free people free people. All human beings crave darkness desperately, but believe it is inappropriate, so we sneak it like a forbidden cigarette, and in doing so, give it a bad reputation. The darkness is actually the feminine, the wild, uncultivated parts of ourselves. Held against this masculine background of laws, rules, and order, the darkness is everything we do not want to be. It is therefore vital—not just to individuals but also nations—that we recontextualize and exalt all things dark, so that we can begin to enter the world we crave and operate there with skill.

We can do this only when we have wrestled with and converted the various and true aspects of being that may or may not conflict with societal views and massaged them, remaining loyal, always, to what exists inside of us, seeing its beauty and rightness and integrating it fully into our expression. What is inside you is never right or wrong, it just *is*. It's what you do with it that changes *everything*.

When working with the daimonic (the "shadow" self is the darkness particular to you; the daimon is a universal darkness, a wildness shared by all humankind), you must keep in mind that this is the most natural process in the world. Human beings often

*"The daimonic, especially when persistently repressed over long periods of time, can be compared to dynamite: It is powerful, volatile, explosive and deadly if mishandled. When treated properly, however, by an expert with the requisite respect, skill, care, courage and consciousness, it can be a useful, constructive, transformative force."*

~DR. STEPHEN DIAMOND

89

*"If you don't have any shadows you're not in the light."*

~LADY GAGA

crave the dark, the wild, more than they crave the light. Entire cities are built for darkness. Las Vegas, New Orleans, and Dubai were built to break rules and offer all the amenities of the night. It's in our DNA, left over from the caves and the hunt. Don't fight it; learn to use it for energy, for understanding; for life and for art.

The process of coming to know oneself is learning to approve of every unique quality of that self, whether it be viewed by the world as shadow or light, with equal and simultaneous approval. Through this long and steady work, three aspects of the deeper self emerge.

First: If you view your unique qualities with unequivocal approval, they are converted to a beauty so rich and deep that everything you look at is saturated with them. Everything becomes beautiful because that is what is generated from the inside.

Second: Almost as a by-product, a deep level of sympathetic compassion for all beings develops. When we do the work of coming to love the unlovable in ourselves, we love the unlovable in all. In our capacity to love what is unlovable, we begin to grow and evolve that compassion into what it was always meant to be.

Third: In coming to know ourselves, we become firmly planted in a foundational rightness of being. This is a solid and unmovable ground that knows that beyond any public opinion, any threat, any ostracism or casting out, regardless of what happens externally, there is solace in the truth of your being that can withstand any external force. It is an incorruptible aspect of self that confers the meaning of our lives.

## Building Your House of Soul

The house of soul is you, the monastery where you retreat and contemplate, the space where you are safe to become your freest, most desired self. As you dig your basement to build your house, emotion will flood the space like groundwater, feeling at times

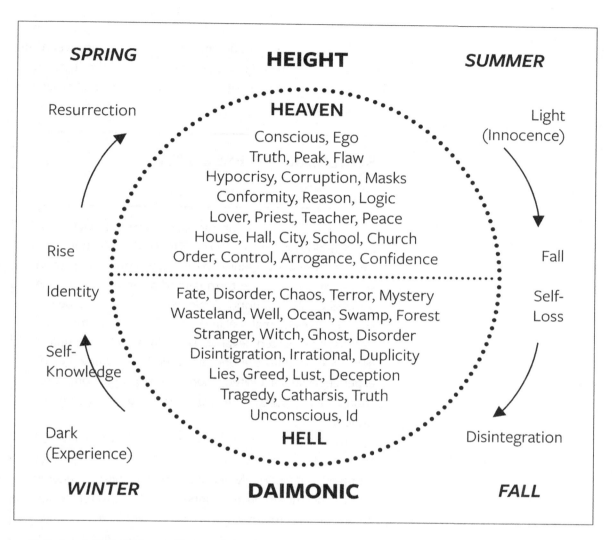

SPRING          **HEIGHT**          *SUMMER*

Resurrection                                                    Light
                    **HEAVEN**                                (Innocence)
              Conscious, Ego
              Truth, Peak, Flaw
              Hypocrisy, Corruption, Masks
              Conformity, Reason, Logic
              Lover, Priest, Teacher, Peace
Rise          House, Hall, City, School, Church                Fall
              Order, Control, Arrogance, Confidence

Identity                                                        Self-
                                                               Loss
              Fate, Disorder, Chaos, Terror, Mystery
              Wasteland, Well, Ocean, Swamp, Forest
              Stranger, Witch, Ghost, Disorder
Self-         Disintigration, Irrational, Duplicity
Knowledge     Lies, Greed, Lust, Deception
              Tragedy, Catharsis, Truth
              Unconscious, Id
Dark          **HELL**                                         Disintegration
(Experience)

*WINTER*        **DAIMONIC**          *FALL*

*credit: Daimonic Circle, by Intractably at English Wikipedia, in the public domain*

that it could overwhelm the project. Feel it. Let it run through your fingers. Cup it in your hands and look. In this way, we use everything that we have and everything that we are in our home, our soul, our sacred space.

That's the excavation work of building a house of soul. You must get down in the dirt, where it is dark, and dig, hauling out stumps and rocks to create where you want to live. This is hard

*Soulmaking: Aligning the conditions of your life so that any request from your soul can be carried out.*

work and sometimes, it's downright scary. Pull up everything your hands touch in the darkness; examined in the light, those old hurts will now serve you. You become master of what was once your ruler.

---

## SOULMAKER'S ESSENTIAL
### *Tumescence*

---

Tumescence is a pocket of psychic energy too powerful for the conscious mind to absorb. (The literal definition is an excited state accompanied by vascular congestion, as in sexual excitement. The term is used as an analogy to the process of stuck emotion.) Negative tumescence begins when undigested material in consciousness, extreme experiences, or repeated negative experiences accumulate and get stuck. When these pockets of undigested energies or experiences are activated, there is a disproportionate response. This backed-up energy is reactive, just waiting to explode.

To the beginner, it feels something like "triggered trauma." For the more experienced, this is the perfect moment to deliberately detonate stuck pockets of energy before the tumescence is unpredictably activated: when we get angry, emotional, or aroused. When we no longer suppress, repress, or oppress arousal, but feel it and convert the energy to something else, we use it as *pharmakos*—from the word *pharmakon,* which is both itself and its opposite: medicine and poison, healer and killer. The advanced soulmaking practitioner uses the whole (arousal, tumescent material, activation, what could or would be dangerous) as the opposite, a bringer of greater life.

Tumescence can be activated in two ways. The first is when a situation occurs that is of the same tone as the situation that caused the block in the first place—something we now avoid, turn away from, or deny. The undigested material is reactivated, and our response is not only to the situation in front of us. It also carries with it all the historical pain and trauma from when we previously experienced it in a similar situation, when we couldn't express what we were feeling.

The second way tumescence can be activated is when a random influx of energy, positive or negative, enters and triggers the existing accumulation. Any time there is an increase in energy (we go to a concert, watch a tragic movie, fall in love) that influx of energy opens the pocket of backed-up pain. We could be suddenly consumed by a memory of loss, a broken heart, or an overall feeling of sadness. We often have the faucets so tightly closed because there is so much backed up energy that the moment anything opens, it can only cause pain.

We have a friend, a high-powered career woman, who says she adds two days to every vacation so she can lock herself in the bathroom and cry. When a little break in her endless carrot-and-stick life opens a window and the tumescence breaks, pain flows out. She feels better, goes for a swim, can't find a towel, and her shoulders begin rising to her ears once again. And round and round she goes.

If not activated, the tumescence can leak in the background, emitting an underlying feeling of irritability and dissatisfaction. If we do not deal with tumescence, we will always suffer from low-grade discontent. It often presents as a complaint, *These things are not enough; I am not enough*, as well as fear and staying small.

Once activated, if the level of energy is stronger than our attention, it will act through us, taking on a quality that is automatic and non-volitional. If you let the tumescence drive you, that's because your attention is not yet powerful enough to meet the force of the activation. You lose your attention when triggered, and your consciousness shoots off into space.

When first learning to pay attention to activation, someone else can play that role for you, the role of conscious seer. That's the job often done by healers, guides, and therapists.

As we learn to identify and activate tumescence, we can cycle back into our system and transform anything into power. A painful exchange with a partner can be drained of its toxins and you can turn it in your mind, finding what is powerful and useful inside it. The pain becomes energy exploded, and a new understanding flows into the space once taken up by the pain. This pain turned to understanding leads to new ideas and creation; the pain now becomes useful. More often though, we do the opposite. Instead of releasing pain and turning it into something else, we constrict or try to block it, because we have no idea there is a way to confront it and, after confronting it, to use it for good.

This tumescent energy can be observed all around. You walk into a store where the salesclerk had an encounter with a difficult customer and that backed-up energy is now fired right at you. Once you walk into it, it becomes yours. What do you want to do with it? Fire the negative energy back and enter into war, or at least a glowering, exhausting stalemate? In that way, the world will pull all your fine creative energy out of you, not giving you a say on how it's spent. That's not useful, and that's not a connection to life. Soulmakers take that tumescence and flip it into something else, saving the memory for a scene in a book or a funny story for a friend. The one thing the soulmaker does not do is take the negative tumescence as their own.

Thus in a society or community, tumescence becomes viral. Everyone is walking into pockets of negative energy and unconsciously reacting to it. It *can* stop with you.

*Tumescence deactivated turns into the creative force unleashed.* The implications are great in terms of individual consciousness and the reintegration and harnessing of energy and arousal. Tumescence is fuel. Further abstracted into culture as a whole, we see the reintegration as a means of healing totalitarianism and dogma in religion, government, and the planet. In other words, what is overly controlling is repaired not by still more rules, laws, fixing, or correction. Broken systems are healed by deliberately allowing nature to flow.

As we descend into darkness, digging into our deepest, most fertile earth, we feel ourselves at the mercy of our bodies and all the instincts and involuntary processes that go with them. The body melts a little wherever it meets the soul: laughing, weeping, blushing, goosebumps, and sexual arousal. We cannot control what we feel, and we cannot always succeed in hiding what we feel. For better or worse, we are on display, impossible to conceal from ourselves or others.

*So Below* is the body where your felt sense, your intuition, lives. *The Below* is the seat of power, a dark, dense, wild place where feminine wisdom lives. *The Above*, the head or brain, is your capital of rational thought. *The Above* is where religion, order, and rules live; it is the realm of spirit and light, but soulmakers tend to love the dark at the bottom of the stairs.

Go down with grace. Surrender to the reality that we can't always choose what we feel, and that there are witnesses to our helplessness. Liberation becomes possible when we stop being so afraid of the involuntary roiling emotions, the loss of control, the wildness inside. Just feel it; you won't die. We can permit ourselves to be spontaneous. We have a greater range of available responses when we begin to include those we censored. And we are true to ourselves. Light and darkness, pure intentions and dark emotion, circle inside and outside of us for all our days. Light and darkness, that is a human being.

*"The intuitive mind is a sacred gift and the rational mind is a faithful servant. We have created a society that honors the servant and has forgotten the gift."*

~ALBERT EINSTEIN

*"Darkness is everything I do not know, cannot control, and am often afraid of. But that's just the beginner's definition. If I am a believer in God, then darkness is also where God dwells. God may also be frightening and uncontrollable and largely unknown to me, yet I decide to trust God anyway."*

~BARBARA TAYLOR

Mother Teresa was described as having an irascible personality while creating a transcendent, world-changing body of work. She was relentless and moved with ease from gutter to palace. There was nowhere she was afraid to go. Whatever darkness was inside of her, whatever anger, whatever fear, she spun it into advocacy and love for the "lowest" of humankind, and her work has rarely been repeated since.

Many charitable foundations were born of great tragedy, saving countless more people through advocacy and awareness. All are examples of spiritual alchemy or the transforming of intense pain into something positive. These people rejected the powerlessness of loss and chose instead to make the world better; they chose to be of positive use. A short list includes the Matthew Shepard Foundation, Susan G. Komen for the Cure, and the Polly Klaas Foundation, all begun by family members in the aftermath of a murder (Shepard), death from breast cancer (Komen), and an abducted child (Klaas).

An invisible force inside humans moves between high and low, good and bad, dark and light, spinning and working its way through consciousness. The people in the examples above took their darkness and transformed it into light, taking noble action. If one dark emotion stays fixed, unless you address it inside, it will rise up to the outside, perhaps causing unconscious impulsive action that, on the mild side, you'll regret and, on the more serious side, might actually cause harm to yourself and others. This is where it all starts to skid, finally coming to rest in places such as a court, a hospital, or perhaps, a prison.

Feel your pain, sit with it. Pull it apart like taffy.

"It's bad," you say, "my pain is bad and I can't do this." You can. Keep paying attention to the pain and as you follow its trail, you'll hit the source. The mother. The father. The ex. The cop. The doctor. The boss. The Man. At that moment, your body will tell you the truth. Your stomach will burn or your eyelids will twitch or your temples will throb. That's the sign you've hit the truth of your pain's beginning and now you can blow it all sky high.

Remember, the "bad" never actually wants to win; it's just a part of the life force, Eros, inside of you. More precisely, Eros is an intimacy with life, an action, an engagement, a process, sometimes misconstrued as sexual. It is an exchange of energy with all things, people, and environments. Life is felt at this moment of impact. Eros is beauty; Eros is life; Eros is connection. Its tools are alchemy, exploding tumescence, activating energy, and working with the daimonic.

Everything demands to be acknowledged and confronted; to be examined, changed, and used. In the eyes of Eros, only a child is afraid to look at the dark and demands only light. Eros has a different aim: to live life on life's terms. And to do this, we must be open to all of it, our monsters as well as all of our shining knights. To merely tamp down, ignore, or subvert the darkness in our lives is to play with a fire that will flare and possibly burn you alive.

Mother Teresa could not transform lives lived on the streets and in the gutters, the poorest of the poor, without knowing those spaces herself. She looked at what many refused to look at and did not look away. She saw no monsters. She began as a witness, because she could. And because her soul in all its transformative power was so great, she acted. She merged with the lowest of the low to teach the world the highest lesson imaginable: unconditional love.

Masters of the daimonic abound. Most often seen in art (the arena of the truest expression of Eros), this process speaks beyond rules, and often beyond words. We feel the truth in our bones. In 1937, when women and children were bombed by Spanish dictator Franco and his Nazi allies at an outdoor market, Picasso painted *Guernica*, a massive canvas that brought the world's attention to the Civil War in Spain. Imagine the emotional horrors Mahler confronted to compose *Songs on the Death of Children*, hauntingly beautiful music of loss and memory.

Jimi Hendrix, once assigned to clear out tunnels in the Vietnam War, turned that experience into the song "Machine Gun," one of the greatest anti-war anthems ever written. Actor

*"The real warriors in this world are the ones that see the details of another's soul. They see the transparency behind walls people put up. They stand on the battlefield of life and expose their heart's transparency, so others can finish the day with hope. They are the sensitive souls that understand that before they could be a light, they first had to feel the burn."*
~SHANNON L. ALDER

*Set up your life so that it is available for your soul. Soul always takes precedence over the material world; don't let your life act as an admonishing parent to a request of your soul. Put aside the material striving and gains to answer the call.*

*"The eye is always caught by the light, but the shadows have more to say."*
~GREGORY MAGUIRE

Chadwick Boseman used it all, including his own impending death, in a performance in *Ma Rainey's Black Bottom* that will resonate through generations.

You see our situation here. We soulmakers know we are made up of many things, positive and negative, peaceful and violent, connected and alone, but our work is to use everything available for the greatest benefit possible. Horror turns to love and ugliness to beauty in the timeless energy of Eros and the daimonic soul.

## The Descent

Nothing can be built anywhere until we clear the terrain, and your soul is no exception. Before you rise into your calling and move into your newly constructed house of soul, dig. Clear your land. Burn out the brambles bouncing around your head:

> *Everyone says I am not talented.*
> *She left me because I wasn't rich.*
> *If I had only been more beautiful, smarter, thinner, I wouldn't be*
>     *alone.*

That's a child talking. Soulmaking demands an adult, meeting what comes as it comes, never ever hiding from life.

## Integration Exercises

- What are the dark parts of yourself that you would rather no one see?

- Are you greedy, manipulative, jealous?

- What are the things that drive you to feel those things?

- Where do you encounter them in your life?

*"I absolutely feel differently about the purpose of my time spent incarcerated. Rather than dwelling on the past and fixating on how I've been wronged, I look to the future and the healthy habits that will help get me there. It's reaffirmed for me the power and potential that accompany times of hardship and suffering."*

~Thomas Stover, Dillwyn Correctional Center, Virginia

# LOOK DEEPER INTO WHAT SCARES YOU

**Fear is an illusion; as soon as you examine it, fear becomes curiosity. This lesson teaches you how to convert fear to fuel your creative engines and engagement with life.**

Consider this: Fear befriended is desire. Not the outgrowths of fear, but the force of fear itself. When we can know the texture, movement, and contours of fear, we discover a deep, cool, dark refuge. What we call fear is not actually fear, it is the beating of the force against a door that is being refused admittance. Anxiety and panic, the trembling sensation, this is the beating.

Soulmaking requires you to face your deepest fears. If you do not, not only will you always be on the run, but you will not arrive at a place inside of you that is really *you*. You'll make bad choices based on avoidance and withdrawal. You'll let everyone tell you how to live—except you. The stakes are high. It's essential to figure out what you are so afraid of happening.

Our biology has trained us to avoid threats. We compartmentalize, put experiences and emotions in rooms in our mind, lock the door, and throw away the key. Those rooms hold an aspect of self that, without connection to our depths, knows only how to fix, fight, and blame, scrambling to find solutions, adding protective denial, seeking external comfort, or even praying. Fear may try to fight through rationalization and justification, throwing the force onto another in anger. Fear may try to blame, using the vehicle of resentment that says to life and all its aspects: "I would be happy if only it weren't for you."

We often fear our most faithful servants, and nowhere is this truer than the way we react to fear. We meet our emotions with a passive attention, fearing our fear, getting angry at our anger, and feeling sad about our sadness. When we can meet them with the

*"The world I held so closely, she played me like a game, I released and left her laughing to stand on my own two feet."*

~JAMIE WEISE

active attention that would truly, enthusiastically, and lovingly welcome and draw in the emotions, we learn that all things we welcome return the favor by offering the essential gift only they can offer. All these emotions (pain, fear, loss) are here *to teach*, yet so few of us are ready for the lesson. Rather than become absorbed into fear and identifying with or being at the mercy of it, we recognize that it—and, indeed, all things—are here to love us.

When our projected fear is removed, we are inherently magical, gifted, visionary. We are each charged with a calling that if we accept it, draws us so far out beyond who we would know ourselves to be, at such an accelerated pace, we scarcely recognize ourselves after a short period of time being "possessed" by our calling.

Take the fear of death (a big one for most people). You can view death with fear, or as a simple fact. You can say "why bother" and shut down, or you can transmute the fear into fuel and create a big, satisfying life no matter how long it lasts. *Maranasati* (the literal translation means "death awareness") is a Buddhist meditation that reminds us there is an urgency to our spiritual development because we could die at any time. Monks sit with corpses for hours and days, even carrying photographs of bodies to remind themselves, no matter where they are, of how the story ends.

In the alchemical mind, death becomes inspiration to achieve now and to live more, because your time here on Earth is finite, and a mystery. This darkness, this not knowing the ending of the story, plays back and forth with your light, diluting and changing fear into creativity. You can paint pictures of it with everything you do, from writing a libretto to cooking a meal and raising a family.

Fear is a tumescence, trapped and causing roadblocks in your psyche; fear keeps you from seeing and feeling the truth. That's why we dig. Often sight or vision hijacks the deeper experience that could only be felt by vulnerably reaching for the black, rough walls of what hurt you, deep down there in the black basement.

Picasso reached for those walls and ran his hands and soul over them in order to describe, in paint, the horror of bombing

*"Life doesn't frighten me at all*
*Not at all*
*Not at all*
*Life doesn't frighten me at all."*
~MAYA ANGELOU

women and children, the screaming mouths, the twisted limbs. He dragged violence and murder into the daylight for all to see. When a Nazi officer confronted him in Paris with, "Did you paint this?" his clear-eyed response was, "No, you did." That is the courage of a master of the daimonic, the audacity of meeting reality on reality's terms. Talking about genius, Picasso fought a war *with a paintbrush*.

Insight into the nature of reality is a serious and grave responsibility. In the darkness where we encourage you to go, all things must be viewed close-up. You must draw experience into yourselves; it cannot be viewed at a distance.

Ask questions, touch it. Feel it anew. Examine what scares you. Use fear as the starting point of your inquiries into your soul; do not be used by it. You will not collapse, rooting around in the darkness; the poison you find there is always the cure.

## Integration Exercises

- What scares you?

- Why?

- If this is ongoing, can you remember when the fear began? Is it attached to a person or thing? An event? Describe it and how you felt when you first experienced it.

- Take the fear to possible endgames.
  If he leaves me, what will I do?
  If the diagnosis is positive, what happens?

- Where do you feel the fear physically?

- What does it feel like?

- Do different fears feel differently?

*"There is a lot of pain and hurt from childhood and beyond. However, at some point in our lives, we have to stop blaming the people in our past for the way we are today. In the past, we had no choice, but today we have choices. You cannot keep blaming the past for today's choices."*

~Sandra S., Central California Women's Facility

# MELTING FIXATION AND TURNING ON

**"Turn-ons" are the things you do that you love so much, you lose all sense of time and space. You'll explore what you love to do—what transports you—and use it as a doorway to your genius.**

When we are not thinking deeply about the matter, we assume that desire is caused by what we desire. You pass by a store window or leaf through a catalog and see a beautiful sweater. You may or may not actually need a new sweater, but need is irrelevant to your feeling for this particular sweater. Whether or not you need it, you desire it. If asked why, you might describe its desirable qualities: the style, the color, and so forth. Seeing the object happens before you desire it, and you believe the sweater caused the desire: You believe your mind wouldn't have desired it if you hadn't seen it.

When you look at it that way, the power of attraction seems to reside in the object. It's as if the beautiful sweater is pulling you toward itself, compelling you to feel, and making you vulnerable to what happens next. The sweater is controlling you, dictating your actions and emotions. If you can acquire the sweater, you feel happy. If it costs more than you can afford or is sold out in your size, you feel disappointed. Yesterday you didn't even know this sweater existed. Now it has the power to make or ruin your day. We call that desire "fixed," or a "fixation," and until you inject your desires with energy, making them volatile and alive, you stay right where you are: a person pining over a sweater.

Okay, we're exaggerating slightly. You probably don't get that bent out of shape if you can't have the sweater. But you get the drift. In believing that desire is caused by its object, we endow the object with power. When we do that, we experience desire as a kind of anxiety. Taking possession of the object is our best idea

*"If you want to experience eternal illumination, put the past and the future out of your mind and remain within the present moment."*

~ELIF SHAFAK

*"Within its reach, though yet ungrasped*
*Desire's perfect Goal—*
*No nearer—lest the Actual—*
*Should disentrall thy soul . . ."*

~EMILY DICKINSON, FROM "WHO NEVER WANTED—MADDEST JOY"

of how to get rid of the anxiety. Quite often, possession gets rid of the desire as well. Once the object is under our control, it no longer has the power over us that was the very source of its allure. Indifferent to what we have attained, we start the cycle all over again, with some new object of desire.

From very early on, philosophers diagnosed this syndrome as a leading cause of human unhappiness. The "original sin" that got Adam and Eve kicked out of paradise was wanting something they weren't supposed to have. Desire has been in the doghouse ever since. The solution religions and philosophies have often proposed is to curtail desire.

The message is: "Don't want, or at least don't want what you can't have."

Curtailing desire has the unfortunate effect of stunting capacities closely related to it: power, resourcefulness, imagination, and *joie de vivre*. If we could really succeed in eliminating desire, nothing new would be created, and nobody would be born.

The real culprit in human suffering is not desire but one of its imposters: fixation. When we believe that desire is caused by its object, only that object will do. Nothing else appeals to us. Nothing else has the power to delight us. We become single-minded and inflexible in our obsession with acquiring it. The gap between desiring and attaining fills up with agitation. If we are severely fixated, we may end up harming ourselves, others, or even the object itself with the forcefulness of our grasping. On the least harmful end of this spectrum, you will find a great collector, sitting in a room obsessively admiring what he has collected. At its most terrifying, the stalker kills his stalkee.

We forget that we have cast the spell that is enchanting us ourselves and gave the object the power it seems to wield. All the harms that get blamed on desire (overindulgence, craving, addiction, obsession, exploitation, greed) can be traced to this fundamental confusion.

When we get into a potentially harmful state such as craving or addiction, we experience ourselves as out of control. The paradox is that fixation arises from being too controlling. Desire has

---

*"'I am your own way of looking at things,' she said. 'When you allow me to live with you, every glance at the world around you will be a sort of salvation.' And I took her hand."*

~WILLIAM STAFFORD, FROM "WHEN I MET MY MUSE"

a quality of leaning forward and moving out of ourselves, out of a sense of static self-sufficiency. Something in us is afraid of losing our balance if we lean out too far. It's as if we are trying to steady ourselves by grasping onto the object of our desire. Fixating is a way of making the situation stable and predictable. If we are fixated or addicted, we can expect to feel tomorrow exactly the way we feel today.

## Desires and Turning On

When I was young, I had a friend named Maria who came from a large, warm Chilean family. She had a beautiful bike, her most prized possession, and she rode it everywhere. Her love for her bike made it seem to glow; it was the most desirable object on Earth. I wanted that same feeling. In fact, I wanted to feel even more of it than she did. I figured that if I bought a better bike than hers, my bike would glow even more.

I bought one that was top of the line. But somehow its glow eluded me. I rarely rode it, and its presence in my garage began to feel vaguely reproachful, a thorn in my side. I almost came to hate it. In my mind, this was the bike's fault. That's how fixation usually ends up: blaming the object for failing to deliver the joy it had originally seemed to promise.

Another word for Maria's relationship to her bike is "turned-on." It's what happens when you ride the bike, coasting along with the wind in your hair.

What turns on desires is not possession, but engagement. What it desires is never just an object, but a partner in that engagement. Even when what we desire is a thing, if we are turned on, we don't experience the thing as an insensate object. To a skilled mechanic, an engine is almost like a conscious being. It has something like a personality, and repairing it is like engaging in a dialogue with it. To someone who loves to knit, yarn feels almost alive. Every yarn responds differently to the needles, and the knitter's hand makes many fine adjustments to accommodate what the yarn is communicating to it.

*"What is addiction, really? It is a sign, a signal, a symptom . . . It is a language that tells us about a plight that must be understood. "*

~ALICE MILLER

*"The knowledge that liberates you is always within you; The knowledge that binds you is always derived from the outside world."*

~SHIVA NEGI

*"It is always with excitement that I wake up in the morning wondering what my intuition will toss up to me, like gifts from the sea. I work with it and rely on it. It's my partner."*

~JONAS SALK

To turn on is active, and often involves doing something, usually with a certain indifference to the practical outcome. You don't have anything to gain from completing a crossword or Sudoku puzzle, but if puzzles turn you on, you couldn't care less. To turn on is being content to accomplish something meaningless for the sheer joy of doing it. There is a quality of effortlessness about it, even during what might appear to be tremendous exertion, because there is no sense of resistance to exertion. Effort is indistinguishable from desire. Your yoke feels easy, your burden light. And while to turn on is loving to do things, it is blissfully oblivious to the possibility of failure, disappointment, or embarrassment. If it can't do well at what it loves to do, it is perfectly happy to do it badly. To turn on is to sing loudly, even when the singing is off-key.

## Integration Exercises

- What does desire feel like to you? What is the last thing you remember feeling desire for?

- Have you ever wanted anything so much that you felt not getting it would damage your life? What did that feel like?

- Did you get it?

- What happened next? If you didn't get it, what happened?

- What do you love to do? What are your "turn-ons"?

- List as many as you can and add to the list as you go. Fold one activity, one of your "turn-ons," into each day.

"There is only one point in which an inmate has a chance to change this existence for themselves. When they find Hope. When they see within their future a chance to feel like a person again. When someone looks up at them when they walk into a room and greets them with a smile instead of a scowl. When they are reminded of the Hope they can give others, they are empowered. Through this empowerment, they can once again define themselves and their life."

~Ray Corona, Eastern Correctional Institution, North Carolina

# DESIRE REVEALS OUR DEPTHS

## LESSON 8

**"Desires" are to be loved; they are a steadfast guide to life. We have dark desires and desires about what we do in the light. Learn to cycle between the two, skillfully maintaining a tension between these poles, powering energy and creativity.**

Now that you have unstuck your desires from fixation, or the pursuit of a red sweater, you can move it to your new word, turn-ons, and explore the language of you. Desire is your soul telling you where it wants to go next, what it needs, what it craves. If you can tune in to your desires, you will hear your own soul speaking directly to you. The soul is always communicating with us through the sensations in the body and it is speaking the totality of life, that from the most miniscule to the grandest, each element is of consequence, precious, and desired. But it is not until you are in its flow that you can sense how elegant life can be. When you connect to your desire, there is no traffic noise, no blaring television—only you doing what you love to do, feeling in complete accord with the Universe.

The quality of your desires determines the quality of your life or, as they say at graduation, "Aim high. Aim true." The truth and potency of your desire is demonstrated by whether or not you get what you desire. What you have is what you consciously or unconsciously draw in, it's what you, on all kinds of levels, want. Call it the law of attraction or whatever you choose, it is the phenomenon in your reality, from the heartbreak to the riches, from the loneliness to the genius—all the material you have chosen to express the sacred nature of your soul.

Your experience of pleasure and pain, or bland, airless suffering, is determined by how deliberate you were with your power of desire, your magnetism, what you chose to draw in, and how well you developed your capacity to represent what you drew up.

Return to your acre of land. How many red sweaters do you have? Can you let go of fixation and move it to turn-ons like growing vegetables and flowers or having your friends over for a meal? Soulmaking is about identifying and strengthening what makes you irreplaceable, your unique role in life. To exist in this dynamic tension of desire, between the worlds of darkness and light and what lies between, can feel like living with one foot on each side of the equator. A consciousness must be developed to not fall too far on either side, tumbling downward into the daimon, or the opposite, denying the dark by locking it in your mind and remaining always in control. To live in a state of vibrant consciousness is to be in a perennial state of micro-adjustments, spontaneously prepared to answer the call to action or wait and listen for what's next. Living with desire means all of us must be alive. Too much focus on the material world and our flow, the fluidity of life, dies and in the static reality, the day-to-day, zombie-like behaviors take over, and the spontaneous melody of life descends into complaint.

Complaint is sound without music that makes you think you are doing something. Complaint often begins with: "I am so busy. John started school, and I've got to get to the dry cleaners before it closes," a seemingly busy life indicative of nothing at all but, well, busyness. Busyness noise erodes into a background sound and, in an attempt to block it out, you begin to block out the depths of your being, your soul's voice telling you what it wants. This is how pride and oblivion occur, you can't hear the universal movement and do your own thing. Your genius (and make no mistake, you have all the access to it you want) is always the marriage between one's unique depths as expressed in the collective, society, the seen world.

Thus desire becomes creative, or it becomes destructive. Because we do not acknowledge it, it runs rampant and unconsciously. It feeds off of hatred, gluttony, and distraction. It provokes, consumes, and checks out in order to feed. It is marked by

*"Controversy is part of the nature of art and creativity."*

~YOKO ONO

disordered thinking that makes you feel powerless or out of control: reactive. It is the place where you cannot help or keep yourself contained. This is because you have squandered the energy you would need to power your attention and it is being drawn, "captured," rather than plugged in to creativity and directed by you. You would need to draw back into yourself through yoga and meditation, concentrate your consciousness, on digging in your basement and finding other feelings like this one, identify patterns, clean the feelings out, and refocus on your desires.

## Fears We Have About Desire

Fears may naturally arise when we align and begin to be moved by desire. Our fears always have to do with the unknown, and desire always draws us toward it. When harnessed, fear becomes the servant of desire rather than its guardian. The first step is to know and name the methods, the most common of which are:

1. We dismiss our internal voice of desire as untrustworthy and thus alienate ourselves from it, usually because we fear that it's asking too much of us.

2. We develop an immune response to desire based on our unwillingness to let go of a voice left over from somewhere, "You're not good enough, you're not worthy": the idea you are not perfect as you are, sitting here reading this. This delusion is most often held in place by a scarcity consciousness that uses a limited notion of who we are, what resources are available, and what we are here to do. Scarcity consciousness is afraid of toilet paper shortages and no love, despite both being abundant resources.

3. A tit-for-tat consciousness is the idea that we must pay for our enjoyment in kind rather than through the reception and acknowledgment of what we've

received. You can feel the joy of receiving a gift without having one to give back, just as you can give a gift without expecting one in return. All tit-for-tatting leads us to is rejecting what our desires have drawn to us, thus rejecting the gifts of our soul.

4. There is invariably a gap between the substitute compass foisted on us by our culture and upbringing and the True North of our yearnings. If our path is to become ever more who we are, until we realize ourselves as one with all, the desire buried within us will invariably rub against the "one size fits all" programs the external world puts upon us. Soulmaking requires an individual, not a mob.

5. In a world that exalts the rigidity of self-will and control, desire occurs as inherently threatening. It is destabilizing by its very nature. Because it wants to move a being that wants to settle into safety and comfort, desire can overwhelm. It is not the desire that is overwhelming, but desire in the face of a mind trying to maintain a fixed reality. This makes desire feel like "temptation," or something you should not do, when the opposite is true.

6. We fear that opening desire will unleash the floodgates of hunger and appetite. We're afraid that we'll become insatiable and hedonistic; that once we start, we will never get filled. To manage this fear, we pick a substitute desire that feels safer, but still end up with the real thing later because we created a craving by denying what we truly desired in the first place. This leads to the swinging pendulum of deprivation and indulgence.

Desires are not good or bad; they just *are*. It's what you do with them (or don't) that has meaning and consequence. Listen constantly to what your desires are saying. It's not the lover one misses, that's a fixed thing. It's the love. It's the passion, con-nection, engagement, creation. Desire powers creation, so create. That's the essence of all life.

## Integration Exercises

- List the desires that feel strongest today. Focus on *feelings* and *actions*, not things.

- Do you desire quiet or action? Go deeper. Examine how the quiet you crave allows ideas and images to rise inside your mind. Describe them.

- If you desire action and movement, when you move with that desire, what happens? How do you feel? What happens around you? Write it all down.

- Begin to write your visions—the things that inspire you.

- Do you want to have a certain kind of experience? Like work on a farm? Cook a meal for someone? Fly a plane? Have a part of yourself be known?

- Starting to write your visions out helps you feel what they feel like in your body.

*"My faith is what's given me strength, knowledge, and the ability to face this time with a sense of optimism that only having faith can provide. My faith is what gives me drive and motivation to face each day with a brighter perspective. To say the least, my faith figures into living in a prison with everything I do each and every day."*

~Leartis Kamau Maurice Caradine, Mendocino County Jail, California

# BEING WITH REALITY ON ITS TERMS

**Being with reality takes a lifetime of practice. "Being with" means staying with yourself, in your body, even when every nerve fiber is throbbing to flee. This teaches meeting the pressures of life while staying attached to your energy, your power, to you.**

Living in reality means being with reality exactly as it is. Pain has the potential to leech perception, dims your interior lights, and disrupts the energy field of your life force. A hungry, empty mind that is raging at the fact that we have pain sees only a world of perpetual lack. The very cord we use to plug ourselves in to reality is disconnected, wrapped around us, and starts to strangle us, separating us from the infinite power and freedom we would naturally access. Cut off from ourselves, we wander like zombies muttering.

*This moment could or should be other than it is.*

*There is something wrong and if there is something wrong, someone is to blame.*

*Something should not have happened or should not be happening.*

The notion that something is needed, something that is not being delivered, rolls in like a wave. If there is a lack, then you are not getting what you deserve, and the world, other people, and institutions are not delivering on what you are entitled to.

We have a friend, a star on football special teams, who returned kicks like a shot as the stadium roared. When the NFL called, it seemed a natural progression of his talent. But his evening activities led to an assault charge and the end of a professional football career, on the edge of its start. His reaction to this reality shut down his life. He never touched a ball again; he denied his own genius, and his suffering was intense. His sense of entitlement to a future in the NFL created a stiffness or rigidity of mind where blame ruled him for decades.

The normally dynamic, self-filtering system of thought became static and frozen, jammed with the concept that something

*"When we blame, we give away our power."*

~GREG ANDERSON

is wrong, someone is to blame, you are not getting your needs met, and something is being done to you. The "you" who is plugged in, who could respond to your environment, has been dissociated. The you who is tethered to your life's energy and the power that would flow through, the you who is fat with riches, who can employ the power of love to mend the world, who recognizes that it is a true power, has been absorbed into the realm of forgetfulness, drowned in the hallucination of lack. In your mind, you're tripping in a desert, and there is no water for a thousand miles.

To this mind, it will sound like a complete indignity to hear that nothing has ever been done to you. A whole series of automated protests will arise to argue this point, supported by substantiated evidence and culturally inculcated belief systems which were spoon-fed to you to ensure that you would never leave the pack. Yes, there has been heartbreak and violation and upset and death. Yet there is a soul that recognizes not the blithe dismissal of the pain, but the necessity of that experience to not only bring you to the totality of your being, but to see that it was a gift offered to you by the forces as an expression of play. Sometimes they play rough—all the more reason to grow strong.

In the face of this gift that feels like a disastrous curse, the automated mind knows only the alternating current of self-pity and a desire to get even. Away from the power of the energy of life and the resilience it offers, the brittle mind becomes fragile; more and more of life needs to be avoided or non-confronted. The rocks and terrors of the primordial elements of fear, rage, and passion need to be held at a distance, which in turn renders you progressively feebler and your injury increasingly more dire. All of this is an invitation to do the one thing you least want to do and that is employ love. Love, like white wine poured into red, makes the solution clear again.

In Natalie Goldberg's book, *Writing Down the Bones*, she tells a story about a friend who felt shame and blamed an errant father. When she was twelve, he left the family, became a born-again Christian, and embezzled money from churches in three states. This was her personal tragedy. Goldberg told her it was a great

*"We can never obtain peace in the outer world until we make peace with ourselves."*

~DALAI LAMA

*"Reality is that which, if you stop believing in it, does not go away."*

~PHILIP K. DICK

*"Self-pity is spiritual suicide. It is an indefensible self-mutilation of the soul."*

~ANTHON ST. MAARTEN

story, and her face lit up. She realized she could transform her life in a new way—as material for writing. When you set aside the blame and irresponsibility, it's amazing what kind of dreams get realized.

As you meet reality, clear-eyed, the question is, how do I love this? Soulmakers always find a way.

## Integration Exercises

- Take a traumatic event in your life and write down a factual account of what happened.

- What happened in the immediate aftermath? Did you hide? Did you place blame? Did you rage? Did you have a breakdown?

- Who are you as a result? Consider what you'd deem positive, and what you'd deem negative.

- Who could you be?

"Now, *my faith is so strong that I'm at peace; He has given me five kids in all, led me from the dark, made me a good dad and role model. And showed me I will be okay, my family will be okay, and that there has to be this balance I never had with prayer and meditation. I continue to grow spiritually and at the age of forty-three, have a whole new set of eyes to look into the Soul and just be thankful, loving, caring, willing . . . so I'm ready to take on the next phase in this crazy thing we call life.*"

~Austin Neuroth, North Kern State Prison, California

# THE NEVER-ENDING DANCE LESSON 10

**Managing fear is a soulmaker's maintenance work; it is a never-ending process. Entering your life without conditions (the endless brain-jockeying we do in hopes we'll get our desired outcomes) unblocks stuck energy, or tumescence, liberating creative energy to flow.**

Our fear and anxiety demands continuous attention. As we expand and say yes to new things, fears will inevitably arise. If we do not stay with these fears, they pile up, and we accumulate debt. If we stay with fear and anxiousness and feel it in the moment, we discharge it so it doesn't back up. If we do not, and instead we disconnect, when we reenter a feeling of fear and anxiety, all the undigested moments of terror have built up and are coming at us. We are triggered. "Triggered," a pop culture term that sounds like Roy Rogers' horse, implies that being inside the terror of fear is easy. It is not. It requires everything we have. But there will be a point where we accept that we have no other option. Because if we do not, we will destroy ourselves or disappear behind the fears and dread, and how can we live a beautiful life like that?

To live a truly awake life, we do not have the option of not feeling fear. We do not have the option of hiding behind a sensation or having any armor up. If we stay with the fear, we have to feel things. If we don't feel them, we risk the harm of blowups and violence "out of nowhere," bad decisions, hurt relationships, and broken vows. We stay with our fear and anxiety. We must. Our focused, calm aim, and sustained attention is vital here.

*"Find out what you are afraid of and go live there."*

~CHUCK PALAHNIUK

## Enter Your Life without Future Conditions

The tumescent fear-boggled mind lives for outcomes. It is always trying to outwit reality. Locked into a world of if/then, fear and anxiety scramble to align themselves with actions they imagine would carry us to a desired end. We behave in strange ways, chasing our perfect ending. The truth is, we have no idea whether that desired end will be desirable once we get there. We always think we know despite the fact that we don't know. The future is opaque, and we sacrifice the process for an always uncertain outcome. We are blind to our myopia.

We imagine that if we leave our lives for an imagined future, only then will we finally know satisfaction. In truth, only by being fully in our lives at this moment can satisfaction occur. It escapes us totally that we could simply forego the projection, start right here, and enter our lives exactly as they are. However, this requires a confession no one wants to make: "My mind is locked up tighter than Fort Knox because I'm afraid of just about everything." Cue the jeering! Yet many walk about in just such a condition, their minds like a giant Store-It-And-Go with floor after floor of locked boxes behind locked sliding doors. The sign behind the eyes says "Full Up" and there's no room for new information.

Managing outcomes is both impossible and a waste of energy. Were we to remain in our center and do nothing, we might allow ourselves to, in humility, be moved. If we let reality come, we might experience the mystery, be delighted and enriched, connect and love. We might just wind up in the exact right place. The natural mind is not about doing nothing, it is about doing everything that needs to be done, and nothing extra.

*"Everyone has a plan until they get punched in the mouth."*

~MIKE TYSON

Allowing ourselves to let go into the flow of experience, however, is seen as an expense we cannot afford, as there is no time. "I am deeply wedded to busyness and cannot stop." With tumescence, there is the invariable "suggestion" that "I can allow myself enjoyment when I finish this task." The option of enjoying this task or this moment looks too expensive in the face of the perception of the threat of material survival. Enjoyment looks frivolous.

This is the trick of the tumescent mind because enjoyment is anything but frivolous; it is in fact the guarantor of excellence and sustainability. Reward, meaning, and enjoyment are then sucked from all experience or are, in best-case scenarios, fleeting. They carry with them the burden of obligation to do the next thing.

So you stand in the shower, delicious warm water sliding down your back, and instead of letting your body have its moments of

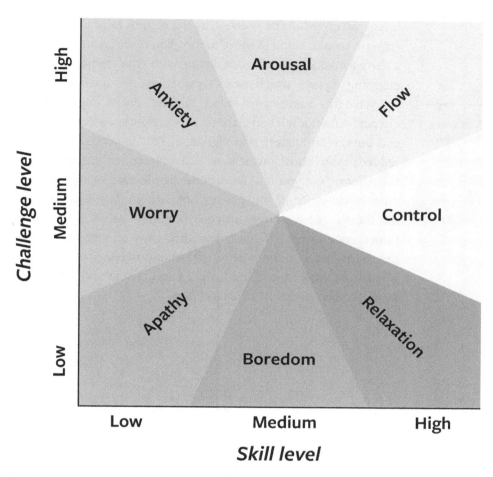

*Challenge vs. Skill, showing flow region, by Oliverbeatson at English Wikipedia, in the public domain*

pleasure, you're thinking, "After this I'll dress and feed the kids, and drive everyone, and swing by the store for cheese, and head back for some Zooms and . . ." And you just blew your chance to have a nice, relaxing time in the shower.

Procrastination, as a product of the tumescent mind, is the result of feeling the world as an unceasing wheel of obligations, drawing out the known obligation to keep the unknown next obligation at bay. You are never where you are. Because the tumescent mind deals in scarcity, you cannot "afford" to "spend" time or energy enjoying the process, as the resources of time and energy are seen as being in short supply. You resent going to a party, *a party* for goodness sakes, or sitting with your friend, instead of engaging in play—which is exactly what inspires you back to flow.

What the tumescence mind, jammed on its anger/fear frequency, does not tell you is that it is passively spending your time and energy on anxiety and vigilance. This expenditure is what reduces your consciousness to the scarcity or survival mind. Whether or not you find an experience pleasant or not depends on how full up your mind is, or not. Are you agitated, running the thought or memory through your mind relentlessly? What tumescence won't tell you is spending time on enjoyment feels indulgent, but it is the precise investment needed to move consciousness away from a fixed, rigid mind of fear and anxiety toward living in a state of effortless flow.

## Integration Exercises

- *Maranasati* appeared in Lesson 6, and now it's time for you to add this to your practice. Also referred to as "The Angel of Death" meditation, you can do it throughout the day as you feel internal blocks, flagging energy, or procrastination.

- Sit comfortably.

- Close your eyes and imagine yourself many years into the future, smiling on your deathbed. You're happy. You've had a great life.

- Then imagine that your present body jumps into your dying body, jolting you back into an instantaneous feeling of *gratitude* and *joy*.

- Revel in the feeling of grass beneath your feet, your skin on fresh sheets, or water running through your hands or hair, ecstatic in your lively new body.

- You'll be fully in the moment, alert and in your body, rather than spinning off in your head into unknowable futures.

"So, *needless to say, I am a mess. That is where this program comes in. In the past, I would have cracked but I have learned to meditate. Since the yard has been open, I have been outside doing yoga and meditating, completely cleansing my thoughts, my soul releasing all my thoughts. I've been outside for the better part of two hours and although I felt stressed and overwhelmed and anxious, I feel so much better sitting with myself."*

~Debbie Bailey, Mendocino County Jail, California

# RECOMMIT TO PRACTICE LESSON 11

As you draw closer to the halfway point of these lessons, contemplate your practice and commit to it again. Reread the "Letter to My Soul" and rework the suggestions which speak to you now.

This is our point of no return, halfway through our building project, a home for the soul. We've dug out the basement and surrendered our darkness, turning it over and over in the light of day. We descended where the pain, delusion, and fixation are and came back to the surface, not only unharmed but with clearer eyes, a sense of acceptance for ourselves and every other being.

We've begun to shape the outside views from our house as well. Our one acre of land looks out at long rolling fields melting into the tangled wilds of creation; unconditional freedom to be explored, attended to, and thus loved. Those ideas are the touchstones of the soul. Acknowledge your goodness. Explore the darkness; take fear and roll it in your hands. Once exposed, you can begin to work with all the energy inside of you to create life with all its messy textures and extremes. Commit to practice and recommit to yourself. This is your daily prayer; this is a timeless place for you to return to for the rest of your life.

We are not practicing to be good or even better people, to find peace or even feel less stressed; we are not practicing to acquire new skills or take on the identity of "practitioner."

We practice to liberate the active sentient, intelligent, and life-seeking aspect of ourselves known as Desire. It's not a silence we seek but sound, the sound of our own souls. If we grow still enough, we can here the soul speak. True desire, when activated and followed, becomes an agent for what we most yearn for: a living breathing relationship with the Mystery. Deep within each of us lies a yearning and that yearning is the Mystery seeking itself. When, through care in practice, we offer ourselves—our

*"Practice means to perform, over and over again in the face of all obstacles, some act of vision, of faith, of desire. Practice is a means of inviting the perfection desired."*

~MARTHA GRAHAM

attention, our time, our frustrations, our vulnerability, our inexperience, our not-knowing—in our hearts, we are met with access to what we cannot see.

Where in the outside world we may be confused, irritated, and out of focus, we are granted entry into the interior world wherein lies a living presence, the source that naturally orders, clarifies, vivifies, and feeds that hunger of the heart: the need to know, to touch, to be made whole by this force that surrounds us, now moving us. We come home to ourselves, curing the homesickness that all suffering is a symptom of, and inhabiting our own lives on its own terms.

What are *your* terms? Every time you practice, you reconnect with your own internal system. You listen to what is called the voice, the sense we all have that lies underneath the rules of right and wrong. And that you can turn the volume up on. When we say, "free the mind," it is liberating this voice. But at present, it is so drowned out with conflicting information, with systems weakened from lifetimes of denial and starvation, it can be challenging to hear. But it can be heard. It can be heard as a loyal ally, frustrating at times, capricious at the beginning, demanding, but loyal.

Practice then is where we allow this deep-seated hunger to draw us to sustenance. Listening to our desire, we are changed, informed, emboldened, attuned in the process, in order to access more through this exchange with life itself. The Mystery, the hidden voices rising inside of us and the things we do not know or understand, draws us ever more out of our known patterns, our habits and needs, into the only thing that will truly gratify: the spacious field where we get to see our experience through life's eyes, where the dramas, jealousy, love, passion, angst, isolation, grief, and yearning play out as rich and beautiful textures and sensations. Not problems and obstacles to be solved, but rhythms and notes to be first felt and then played through the instrument of the body. In practice, we sit and watch, and the Mystery wells up with new, inexhaustible energies, sensations, and ideas, a world without end.

*"If you have time to breathe, you have time to meditate. You breathe when you walk. You breathe when you stand. You breathe when you lie down."*

~AJAHN AMARO

*"To practice any art, no matter how well or how badly, is a way to make your soul grow. So do it."*

~KURT VONNEGUT

We develop respect, care, and tending to the body as the instrument through which all experience is known. Each day is a tuning, an inquiry into what would facilitate this pitch-perfect response to life. Not in spite of, but because of and through this body, through its tenderness and frailties, we know life from its most subtle to its most extreme.

## Integration Exercises

- Write about what you felt before, during, and after your practice.

- When has it seemed effortless? When is it difficult?
  For example: "On days I work late, morning practice is difficult the following day," or "My practice feels deeper when I meditate outside in the backyard."

- Can you make any adjustments to your day to enhance your practice?

- Revisit the first nine exercises, and reading them anew, is your regimen still working? Is there anything that wants to change? This is your acre of land.

# PART II

# BUILDING YOUR HOUSE OF SOUL

## INTRODUCTION

The previous eleven lessons were demolition, the essential preparation for constructing your internal life for unconditional freedom. That means your soul is yours, and you are free despite your circumstances. You could be in solitary confinement on Rikers Island or a world cruise on the Queen Elizabeth II and still feel the same inside: free. Congratulations. If you're here, you've done some hard work, facing difficult feelings, memories, and sensations. You've stretched your body and sat and listened to your insides. You've learned to connect to the Mystery in a way you may not yet understand. This is big; feel it with a sense of accomplishment. You are learning to meet the reality of your life. Few undertake the journey, though it is essential for all.

You have dug down into your acre, preparing your land, touching the darkness as you turn the earth, the darkness you hold, that every human holds. Going down into the pain is always the first step in working darkness into beauty. Understanding the darkness inside yourself is essential in understanding the darkness in others. Accepting it all allows you to love it all and from that love, all things are possible. We know because we have seen it, again and again and again.

Now we work on your house of soul, the beautiful interior structure where everything that is you lives and breathes. This is a life's work. This is the building of an interior cathedral, and it must be done by hand—your hand, just as the old builders did it. And then, like the caretaker of any great cathedral, you care for it always, tending to each of its parts, realigning boards that have drifted apart, fixing leaks and rot.

Soulmakers love to build; it's a part of our essence, our calling. And since it begins with the raw power of the soul, we engage hard with this part. It's one of our turn-ons, our desires, in fact.

*"Beneath the rib cage, therein lies a treasure yet to be discovered, but it takes getting out of one's comfort zone to untap the necessary courage. One has to be willing to dig a little deeper than they ever thought they could go and sometimes one has to risk it all if they ever expect to grow."*

~Marlon J. Walker-Walkwek,
California Medical Facility

# THE FIRST ROOM OF SOUL: PERFECTION, NOT PERFECTIONISM

## LESSON 12

**Whether you run a vast empire or sleep on the couch most of the day, you are the same and you are perfect. Nothing ever changes that fact. Knowing this, never chase perfectionism; it destroys life.**

As we work with the energy of Eros, our life force, and the timelessness inside ourselves that we found during practice, we are one with life itself. We are always evolving and growing, finding new forms. Perfection, not perfectionism, is ever moving; we feel it in our bodies, in our bones. Perfection radiates effortlessly: It is our natural state. Perfection is the sound of laughter coming through the wall, birdsong at dusk, sunlight on water. Children and animals exude perfection, so they live in the moment. Darkness comes to us like this as well; we pass a graveyard at noon and feel a burning sensation in the body; a lost loved one connects with our soul. The ache is immediate; it may never go away. Glass and metal litters an intersection; two cars have T-boned at a high rate of speed. As you are flagged on past the wreckage, you reach for your children knowing we are all living one quick instant away from catastrophe.

If we can recognize our perfection, we can afford to venture into the whole of ourselves, the places inside us that are still wild, that haven't been tended and domesticated and developed through our intellect, or through what we have been told about right and wrong or who or what we should be, where there is uncertainty and Mystery. We will make mistakes and get lost, but we learn the language of the parts of ourselves that are hidden, unexpressed. There is no lack of beauty. Eros, the unseen force that animates me, you, and the Universe, offers stunning endowments

*"Perfectionism is the voice of the oppressor, the enemy of the people. It will keep you cramped and insane your whole life, and it is the main obstacle between you and a shitty first draft. I think perfectionism is based on the obsessive belief that if you run carefully enough, hitting each stepping-stone just right, you won't have to die. The truth is that you will die anyway and that a lot of people who aren't even looking at their feet are going to do a whole lot better than you and have a lot more fun while they're doing it."*

~ANNE LAMOTT

*"Perfectionism is self-abuse of the highest order."*

~ANNE WILSON SCHAEF

to help us realize how beautiful life is, even when it seems ugly and harsh. It allows us to see through our judgments and be filled with a magnetism that connects us with what is around us. We feel the draw, the pull, the call.

Convention fixates on perfectionism. The fixation on perfectionism has us convinced that if we just do more, then happiness is right around the corner. Make more money so you can buy a bigger house. Look perfect to the neighbors. Consume. Buy trendier clothes to keep up with the "girls." Well we don't have to keep up with anyone because we already know our perfection. We feel it when we sink down into our bodies in practice. Some part of us already knows. The friction between perfection and imperfection signals a desire to uncover a deeper love, to embrace our potential for growth, becoming, of finding meaning and purpose.

Perfectionism is the antithesis of perfection. Conventional logic says that something cannot both be something and not be something at the same time. Life is the bridge that says both can be true. Perfectionism is held inside of perfection, not the other way around. Perfectionism is what happens when we cut ourselves off from the life force. We begin an endless attempt to recreate the conditions of perfection, which we can never capture, never grasp, to which we can only surrender.

Heartbreaking stories of individual characters colliding with perfectionism fill theaters and libraries, in every language and every country around the world. Perfectionism is Tragedy. In almost every example, they are destroyed by a thousand cuts of the soullessness of expectations and manners. Literature is filled with these stories of perfectionism. A woman, deeply engaged with her life as an artist, becomes pregnant and moves to the suburbs to raise a family; she goes mad among the violently manicured lawns and unspoken norms and rules, finally committing suicide. Her husband and child are left behind to stare at her huge canvases and wonder.

A Russian bureaucrat's agonized death cries fill his fine house, and in his torment, he understands how useless his life was, filling out ledgers and forms with precision. His passing is marked only by those lining up to take his job.

Other victims of perfectionism? Just look around.

Stop chasing perfectionism and find perfection within every moment of every day; a friend's gap-toothed smile, getting stuck in the subway with a funny stranger, children running and squealing at the top of their lungs. That is the stuff of perfect life, moments and images unspooling as we go, listening, adjusting, and being in flow.

What will you do inside your perfect first room?

## Integration Exercises

- Where do you get caught in perfectionism? Where do you not?

- What would be different if you sat in your perfection?

- Would you be more accepting of yourself? Others?

- What would that look like?

*"When I act bored, ask me to play a game or give me a suggestion of something I can do in a small group. When I become depressed, remind me of the positive things going on and that my bad karma is being extinguished. When I become angry, remind me I'm being tested and that I have the resources to handle/pass the test."*

~Michael Wright, Saguaro Correctional Center, Arizona

# WIRING THE HOUSE FOR FEMININE POWER

## LESSON 13

Stop fighting and use your power. This lesson explores feminine power versus masculine force. We train our language so that others hear us, never shouting or demanding to be heard. The ultimate power is knowing who we are, restoring ourselves, inspiring, and employing the ultimate force on earth: Love.

True power does not fight anything; it is not oppositional. If there is a fight, or a struggle, we are still in the training ground of developing power. Power is the opposite of force; it does not fight against anything. Power gives power, it self-generates. Power defines new and more effective ways and means with generosity, because power recognizes an "us" to all things. In martial arts, power would be best represented by *aikido*, a Japanese invention whose intention is to not injure the attacker. Rather the energy of the assault is deflected and converted to a connected energy with the aikido defender. In that way, violence becomes dance, and no one is hurt. Again we see it: Darkness becomes art.

Power is responsibility, a responsibility willing to ensure that the listener can understand us; we must speak in their language or train them in ours. To do the real work of power is to understand that culture is trained that emotionality and expression are childlike. The "feminine" way of presenting, the choosing of power over force, is demure and innocent.

To be women who can be heard then, is to find our feminine power, to own our language and then train others how to hear it. We can complain about the labor of this, but this is the labor of real love. Love with power. Love that is determined to build connection because that is what true power does.

There is no room for resentment that "they don't get it." Who did we think was here to teach men if not us? To say it is men's responsibility to learn our language, to see our power, and to get angry when they don't—that is what is childlike. It is our responsibility to demonstrate it in such a way that it is undeniable, first

*"I am not free while any woman is unfree, even when her shackles are very different from my own."*

~AUDRE LORDE

to ourselves and then to the world; this is the journey of all the marginalized. To bring forth what we have to offer, this is the path of initiation, to figure out how to be seen and heard in an incontrovertible way. We don't fight anyone; we stand firm in our power and continue speaking until we are heard. This will require you to put in the work to understand your desires and say whatever it is you need to say. That's a soul in power.

Figuring out how we communicate this means figuring out how to weave it into the world. We are not getting anything from the male-configured structures, a "you versus me" series of oppositional forces. To be honest, the "male-shaped" power organization does not have much; a broken world where he is being circled by a lot of angry people who want to tear down the system with no alternative suggestion. We want to bring something to man. We want to bring what will heal, grow, evolve the world, and man himself. That is a woman's power.

Man produces—as simple as man produces sperm. But woman creates; she creates life. When a woman accepts the awesome nature of this reality, when she truly takes it in not as a weapon, not as a means of saying "see!" but when she rests inside of that power, she will likely see man relieved and rejoicing, simply because this is the weight of the truth that—in our denial of it—they have had to hold.

And man produces. He simply does. But a man is at his best when he is producing for someone. When a woman in her power is a muse, man is genius; he rises to her art. When she is absent, he builds without guidance. The creative is missing. We end up with cold production, factories, and cement. And yet we blame him for our absence, our unwillingness to rise to the level of woman that could and would inspire this greatness in him. When we speak, we whine, yell, or complain; if we want something, we ego-stroke, placate, or submit. We live looking at what we can get and what we lack.

This is not a woman in her power. Woman in her power is deeply seated in what she can bring forth. But she must bring it forth from the feminine plane, and the feminine plane is not

*"You can waste your lives drawing lines. Or you can live your life by crossing them."*

~SHONDA RHIMES

the spiritual but the erotic; it is filled with vibrant pulsating soul. Woman in the spiritual plane is infantilized, virginalized, untouched by life or power. This woman will always be—at best—a rib in man, but she will never be sovereign. She will never be a companion. She will never be a counterpole that balances life. She will be a possession, not an inspiration. To meet and match him as friend, as the creative force that he produces for and from, she must inhabit her own domain. Then she can bring it forth as the full complement.

"Hard" power must have a foe, something to bend to its will. That is not the way of feminine "soft" power, which says, "The seat of power is my soul, knowing who I am and how I feel." "Soft" power knows the ultimate force on earth is love.

## Integration Exercises

- As someone who identifies as a woman, man, or otherwise, what does feminine power look like to you?

- How does it show up in your life? In the world around you?

- What would the world look like with more feminine power?

- What are the ways you can support more feminine power in your life?

"I feel like I belong in a special place in this world. I believe I have a purpose in this life even though I am going through hard times right now. I just bring out my genius and I feel much better. This program made me believe in humans again. I feel like I can let my walls down and be vulnerable without being afraid so I just expose myself. This program made me feel like I got someone to lean on. I also feel protected and loved. I also learned that love is the only real thing."

~Jose Mendoza, High Desert State Prison, California

# DECORATE YOUR ROOMS WITH DESIRES

**When desires meet reality, responsibility and consequences occur. It takes experience mediating between the two. This lesson embraces adulthood and harnesses desires with reality so that you may live in your highest calling, creation.**

Working with desire is simple, but not easy. It requires a diligent and consistent focus and development of a consistent, inquiring, ambient attention. What this looks like is having a sense of our True North. Our True North is a place where, even for a second, we have felt free from the narrative mind, the confines of time, the pressure of the body, and have sensed effortlessness, depth, beauty, and being moved in each moment. We sense whether whatever is entering our consciousness will bring us closer to that sense of freedom or away from it. This is not to be confused with escapism; here we are setting our compass toward liberation.

Desire is a power we all share, just as we all share human suffering. Desire asks us to live from a deeper drive, not where we merely follow orders, execute, and comply with a particular idea of how to be. Instead, we are invited into a level of adulthood where we must learn experientially by trying things out and facing consequences, rather than relying on what an external authority might tell us, absolving us of the responsibility of knowing. Desire demands *experience*.

To engage in freedom is to sit in front of a keyboard, telling your story without the constraint of time, and you look up stunned that the sun is setting. A pilot touches the edge of a cloud and decides to investigate, abandoning linear flight to spin through glistening water drops and ice crystals that form cathedrals in the sky. A reader finishes *Anna Karenina* and her heart drops, heartbroken Anna and her lover Vronsky have left the room. You meet an old friend for coffee and look up to see that three hours have passed.

*"Whenever you are creating beauty around you, you are restoring your own soul."*

~ALICE WALKER

*"Our desire is to grow so quiet and to work so deeply that we participate fully in the mystery in which we're embedded. When we manage to do that we feel as if we have merged with the universe; for the duration of that experience we feel immortal."*

~ERIC MAISEL

At any given moment, we are maintaining a steady stream of alive, open, and spacious sensation, using that as our guide and moving toward or away from phenomena based on how closely they match this sensation of desire. If we continue to focus here regardless, our programmed preferences shift. What we think is attractive or repulsive does not always match up with our internal sensory magnet. What we perceive to be our limitations are often constructs, not of our being but of our minds. It may be time to stop before we want to, or a place to continue where we otherwise quit, but we are either in it or not. It is binary in that way.

All excellence, relief, genius, and ultimate liberation comes from simply sensing and responding to this single, felt sense-memory of freedom, building our entire consciousness around it, to create an attention that is resilient, flexible, and subtle enough to remain with regardless of the conditions of the mind or our environment. This is our refuge. But it is a refuge that requires eternal and vigilant maintenance because this refuge is True North, a most precious and sacred place.

Every time you engage with your truest desire, the True North, where you are so turned-on and alive there is no time and no space, you engage with the eternal. That is how you connect with the soul and carry it outward into the timelessness of all creation.

## Integration Exercise

*Soul Dating*

With True North in mind, grab a friend, a lover, a mate. Your mission here is to introduce them to one of your desires, your "turn-ons," one that feels particularly good and right at this moment on this day. In this way, we reveal ourselves and teach others to live inside their truest meaning, a glowing individual connected to the whole. When you operate in concert with your desires, you become full up with life; you feel satisfied. Abundance overflows into the other and fills them with more and more energy, more life. Write about the day, paying close attention to how you light up—or come alive—and how your companion lights up as you move through your "date."

"I've noticed that due to my daily yoga meditations I am not as stressed and tense from my workload and the various other assignments I do throughout the day. I find that my mind is clearer and I am more relaxed, thus I'm sleeping more soundly throughout the night. Yoga and meditation are my new way of unwinding at the end of the day."

~Nora Igova, Central California Women's Facility

# REBOOT CONSTANTLY: RECEPTION

## LESSON 15

**Practice methods to increase your attention, staying more closely attuned to everything around you. Five simple instructions help you stay connected to life, meeting everything with calm, clear eyes.**

*"If you have a body, you are entitled to the full range of feelings. It comes with the package."*

~ANNE LAMOTT

When we begin working in earnest inside the house of soul, it quickly becomes obvious that we must hone our attention to develop the skills to listen to every incoming message, recognize it, be with it, and be moved by it. That's how you attend to reality. That's how a newly minted alchemist spins whatever materials you encounter into gold.

Your ability to receive is based on the care of your attention, by going down into the body and listening. Your body *knows*. It knows everything there is to know and will not let you down. Feel it. That's why you practice daily as well, to extend the muscles of your stillness and attention further and deeper into your life. First you will need to adopt *approval* for what you feel and hear and see. It is an acceptance of reality. Approval is the ability to see the full spectrum of life, the willingness to engage with it and love it no matter its content. Admit and look at what *is* directly in front of you without agreement with it. You could watch a huge protest, one outrage or another marching by your window, and not agree with the cause. However, you must approve of the march; it is happening, and the marchers have an inalienable right to a voice, to speak. You approve while not being in agreement. We develop intuition by learning to actively receive the directions we hear, no matter how subtle, nuanced, or mysterious they are.

Reception is distinct from projection, which may include fantasy or imagination. If we are projecting, we are not receiving. If we are passively receiving, then we are only receiving into our default preformed ideas. Intuiting requires us to be prepared for the unknown, to relax into uncertainty as we listen with curiosity and possibility. Intuition requires approval.

As musician Tina Turner sought ways out of the pain of her marriage and her life, her sister suggested she chant in the tradition of Nichiren Buddhism. She did until her soul grew so much power, she walked to the edge of the stage and began chanting, "*Nam Myoho Renge Kyo*" as Ike and the band stood confused behind her. Tens of thousands of souls exploded back at her with one voice rising above all others. Her soul said, *Tina, you're receiving.*

She finally *heard* herself, her own intuition. She left Ike soon after.

We explore intimacy through our relationships with the things around us. When we allow ourselves to be permeable and accessible, we can enter other worlds and let them enter us. We can develop the ability to feel a moment in its full expression, tremulous or bright, strong or soft, vibratory or smooth, to be fully present, open and engaged with both our internal and external worlds. We can feel and relate to anything and everything that we experience. The empathy that we feel when there is this resonance is intimacy. We only harm that which we cannot feel.

*Power* is the ability to stay conscious and maintain volition in the face of programmed behaviors, the ability to use attention to direct or organize psychic energy. This is not defiance or rebellion, though that may be part of it. Real power comes when we can change what is around us through our presence alone and then have volition, a choice, as to whether we will be changed by our conditions. Power is the force that drives you to turn on the camera and keep filming; power does not look away.

At the core of our being is a consciousness that allows us to go anywhere; it has endless optionality. Imagine a long, long hallway with many doors; that's your mind on optionality. You have a choice. You have choices. Lots of them. Those are the doors. Walk through whichever one you choose. Optionality provides access to all our gifts, the full spectrum of our potential, where we feel the most ourselves. That is ultimately what we are seeking: that

"*All truths are easy to understand once they are discovered; the point is to discover them.*

~GALILEO GALILEI

"*Everything in life that we really accept undergoes a change. So suffering must become Love. This is the mystery. This is what I must do.*

~KATHERINE MANSFIELD

sense of everything being open and limitless. From this location, we can have every part of us available. It is a dynamic state of consciousness in which possibilities become numberless.

Approval, intuition, intimacy, power, and optionality are the five key elements of reception that, when functioning together, create a connection to reality that presents endless open possibilities rather than fear and constriction.

You'll see all of reality as something with value, something to use. Soulmakers look at a dirty alleyway and imagine a photo shoot with a snow-white dress. We view a person on death row as a mentor, providing a transformational lesson in humanity. We are open to all of experience and notice the good and the difficult. We accept all of it. In fact, we welcome it and dive in. That's how we live in our full power; we are completely alive.

*"Intimacy is not something that just happens between two people; it is a way of being alive. At every moment, we are choosing either to reveal ourselves or to protect ourselves, to value ourselves or to diminish ourselves, to tell the truth or to hide. To dive into life or to avoid it. Intimacy is making the choice to be connected to, rather than isolated from, our deepest truth at that moment."*

~GENEEN ROTH

## Integration Exercises

*Scan Your Body*

- Lie down comfortably, putting pillows underneath the knees and head, if you'd like.

- Starting at your feet, focus on how they feel. As your thoughts center there, what do you notice? Do your feet grow warm? Do the soles tingle?

- Now move up, focusing on ankles and asking yourself the same question.

- From there, it's on to the calves, knees, and so on until you reach the crown of your head. Notice sensation.

- If the thought, *How will I pay the mortgage?*, pops into your head while focusing on a painful neck, you'll see how your reality lives in the body.

*"I want to get to love myself so I can love others as well. This is going to take some time and I'm willing to use this time to change the way I look at myself as a person."*

~Keñya Delgadillo, Mendocino County Jail, California

# THE LABOR IS ALWAYS LOVE    LESSON 16

**Explore more deeply the idea put forth in your first lesson of soulmaking: You are perfect and perfectly made for love. To believe yourself unlovable is to deny reality and drink the Kool-Aid society heaps on you. Explode that notion for good.**

Some argue that everyone wants to lose but that some will fight to the death over it. Like an octopus with many arms, many expressions, but the belief at the foundation is that *I am not lovable.*

This single core belief drives a whole set of behaviors that fuel the old-guard culture. The theater we see play out on the political stage all boils down to this, but only a few will follow the thread to get to the core from which a world of reactivity comes to flip that switch. If you believe yourself to be unlovable, odds are you will try to prove that to be true. Most will remain in a private conversation with this belief and react to it in a whole variety of ways from, *I am not lovable therefore I have to get mine from forcing my way*, to the demands of the victim identity for others to conform to make them comfortable, rather than developing resilience.

Other beliefs that follow are: *I am not lovable unless I produce, therefore I will drive myself into exhausted misery never giving myself to others and bringing intimacy*, and, *I am not lovable and must therefore retreat to protect others from me, because my mask will fall off and they will see the hate or the wildness inside myself that I deem evil.*

You can find yourself building resentments and the growing notion that if you stopped serving the desires of others, you would be of no value whatsoever. You drive an extra carpool, hands clutched angrily to the wheel. You cover for the guy who couldn't figure his way through the report and find out he went out to dinner while you typed. You may do things you really don't want to do with the idea you'll get "points" from people.

Often we see people living lives in service to this belief, arranging their worlds to support it, working in place rather than offering their hearts, turning work into toil rather than play and creativity. People keeping their deepest selves and desires

*"Anytime you try to be a loving person, you're doing your part to save the world."*

~MARIANNE WILLIAMSON

hidden, even from themselves, locked down under either a layer of propriety or misery. People finding ways to push everyone who would love them away as confirmation that, "See? Nobody stays."

It becomes so woven into the consciousness that people are driven to either prove that they are beyond love, or that they deserve to be loved with an emphatic demand. We seek outward for what can only be realized inside. The culture's job is to teach everyone how to make this journey rather than only offering ways to imprison, medicate, distract, and protect those who have not made the journey. Everyone must be given the tools and the guidance to make this journey, or we die.

When you believe yourself to be unlovable, you reject reality. When society says, "Drink this and forget about it," society lies to you. Examination and clear-eyed exploration of your insides is the only way to make this right. Understanding what you believed and why you believed it is the only way to see the lie.

A lack of self-love is found everywhere, from a person marginalized on the very edge of existence to the overachieving Wall Street banker with unknown riches. If they have not been inside themselves and proven that they can love themselves, then no one can prove it to them. Those who view others as untrustworthy rarely trust themselves. Those who view others as needing constant monitoring often view themselves as fundamentally dangerous. The judgmental spend their lives critiquing themselves. We are merely seeing their insides overflowing into the outside.

Our inquiry into ourselves and our own *I am unlovable* thoughts are part of a journey into the unknown. It cannot start with pat answers: "Of course, we are all lovable," or "God is love." It is a question in each of our hearts, there to draw us down and in.

Self-inquiry will require all the qualities we would need to be a loving human being, creative and contributing, self-possessed and filled with experiential self-knowledge. Love does not emanate from a mind filled with self-loathing, self-berating, other-pointing, shame, guilt, or self-doubt. We have not trained people that it makes no difference if we are anxious and beating

*"Perhaps they are not stars in the sky, but rather openings where our loved ones shine down to let us know they are happy."*

~ESKIMO LEGEND

*"I am not looking to escape my darkness; I am learning to love myself there."*

~RUNE LAZULI

ourselves up or beating someone else up. Violence transmits lovelessness everywhere. There is no place to hide.

Love is an emanation. If the internal voices are not loving, the external voices, no matter how well-disguised, will not be either. We have been trained by culture that we can pretend to take the right action over internal rot. It does not matter what we do if we are not rooted in love, which does not mean that we cannot experience fear. It is not about love or fear. It is love *with* fear. We cannot neglect the self and be loving. And yet, to love oneself is not a platitude or indulgence; it is not a retreat; it is a righteous activity of going more and more deeply into the core that is love and converting that. To be clear, it is only self-love if it includes the love of others. There is no "I love myself" that is in contradiction to loving others.

We have missed the nexus point. Society at best has trained people that we can only get our exchange of love with the impersonal, abstract God or with the material world. We have not trained people in the exchange of love with the flesh, the beating pulse, the dangerous world of the people around us. People who could hurt us, who require something of us. We so desperately want it to be out there, just beyond the sound barrier of risk and heartbreak and jealousy and the sensitivity of our humanity. We want to learn how to love what is outside, when love is the product of loving our insides.

Given the above, you can see that loving oneself will save the world; that's what soulmakers do. We love inside and carry it outward and in so doing, we change the world.

*"Love pouring out of you is evidence of God pouring into you."*

~MATSHONA DHLIWAYO

*"In order to love who you are, you cannot hate the experiences that shaped you."*

~ANDRÉA DYKSTRA

## Integration Exercises

- Start by loving one part about you: your one green leaf. Is it the way you care for your family? The way you show up for your work?

- What is one thing you love about yourself?

- Do this daily for a week. Find one new thing about yourself internally that you love.

*"My negative self talk got the best of me for a bit. So, what I did instead is started writing a curriculum for The Art of Soulmaking classes that I want to lead in-person. I made posters and class folders, and I even wrote a contract for the class. I picked out quotes for every week to read on the board. I purchased yoga meditation music to play during class. I got lavender to boil in class with a stinger in water so the classroom would have a calming scent."*

~Jessalynn Graham, Central California Women's Facility

# PLAY IN EVERY ROOM

# LESSON 17

As you've grown stronger, start to play. Stretch yourself. As "challenges" arise, don't see them as problems; see them as opportunities to learn. Say "yes" without knowing where you'll land. You can handle it. Risk— that's how you grow.

We associate discomfort with "problem." Where there's smoke, there's fire, right? We then say that wherever there is discomfort, we expect a problem. The existing model of thinking is that we feel discomfort, look for the problem causing it, and seek out a solution. This is how the rational mind frames things. The link is inextricable.

But what if it is not that way at all? What if discomfort is not a sign of a problem but a call for expression, creation, and what is called *funktionlust*—our being in our purpose? For humans, this is to play: the act of being totally engaged in what we are doing now. Synonyms are being in flow, reaching a flow-state, or engagement with purpose.

When you approach life like a game and play with it, everything changes. The whole game might suddenly reveal itself; the wizard might come out. We might see behind the masks of the noble ones, in Washington, DC, in your boss's office, or at the homeowner's association. You will find those players deeply invested in maintaining the illusion of the problems they solve. We might discover that often, the cures are the cause of the issue, or create another one. We might discover that research, with respect to pathology, is not benign; that it is a cause of the very pathology it is researching. How could a government approve a drug to combat pain and kill almost a million people? Easy, and the United States did it with Oxycontin, its doctors prescribing away. Oxy was about saving the healthcare industry billions as it cycled its patients out of the hospital with a vial of pills the very same day as major surgery.

We might discover that "positivity" is simply another mutation of the same mind that says something must be done about the problem. We might be faced with a deeper question:

*"Scientists have recently determined that it takes approximately 400 repetitions to create a new synapse in the brain, unless it is done with play, in which case it takes between ten and twenty repetitions."*

~DR. KARYN PURVIS

If there is no problem to fix, what would we do with ourselves? How would we find meaning and motivation to get out of bed each day?

Rising to meet problems day in and day out creates a fragile tentative mind that holds to the side of the pool, afraid to let go and express, create, and play. We might notice that the notion of levity and fun and humor sounds irresponsible, and responsible is good. We want to be good. And there are all of these enemies and demons and sicknesses and traumas that must be faced. Once they have been appropriately dealt with, then perhaps we could consider playing. Maybe then souls would unlock, and more nimble heads could imagine a way to alleviate pain without Oxy, a problem created by trying to solve another problem.

Why are we so fixated on the "problem/solution" way of living? Is that really the mindset required to approach each day? The force of life might suggest something you perceive as a "problem" is just energy that got locked in because it was labeled a problem in the first place. When you fight about loading a dishwasher, you call the other's methods a "problem," and it's on, the verbal nitpicking back and forth. But the grand potentate left no definitive instructions on the dishwasher, so there is no wrong; you are fighting something else. You are fighting blocked energy. Problem energy often arrives through the vehicle of shame, created by the idea that "something is wrong."

This was in turn created by the idea that if we do not identify what is wrong, then wrong things will continue to happen, never mind the fact that the "wrong" things keep happening the more we look for them. Life responds that while a trauma label is hugely satisfying to the identity, it is not beneficial to your essence, the holiest center of you. All this searching for problems is the problem; you are fixated and fixed (tumescence).

This model may allow us to fixate on an identity, but it can never bring us to true joy, the joy of seeing that there has never been a problem. This is not because we are in denial. We are looking it square in the eye, and not because we are "healing" or have healed. It's not because we are delusional or disassociated or positively thinking about it. It is because there is, and was, no problem.

The pathologies we feel in ourselves and see in others are, for the most part, the result of the repression-expulsion response: push the thought down or deny it outright. This is not cured but caused by the mind that labels expression a problem and thus limits expression.

Creativity unexpressed as creativity expresses as violence and destruction. Let it be clear that the suggestion is never to excuse violence and head toward an unconscious free-for-all form of hedonism and animalistic consumption. That is an outgrowth of an overly restrictive mind that is repugnant to our life force.

What is different in the life of the soulmaker is that we recognize what that energy wants to do, and we understand we can employ it viciously or with virtuosity. We find consistent ways and means for that energy to be employed in what would bring it the greatest joy. Soulmaking does this rather than having it build up, explode, and be wasted.

Violence and violation are simply creative energy poorly employed. Our life force is the master that accepts the animal is going to, and must, play. Rather than punishing it for its nature and seeing it as a problem, life takes the position of good master or mistress, finding ways for that energy to express. What is then brought about is a state of eudaimonia, or human flourishing. The same energy is consciously employed in the realization of our gifts, rather than the endless, self-perpetuating cycle of solving problems.

> *"Play is the brain's favorite way of learning."*
>
> ~DIANE ACKERMAN

## EUDAIMONIA

The term *eudaimonia*, first used by the ancients in Greece, is the perfect state of living. Eudaimonia is authenticity, excellence, meaning, and growth—a state of human flourishing that occurs when we are thriving in the spot of our soul. Eudaimonia is the skier having the run of her life, the painter so deeply engaged with his creation that all other issues fall from his mind for hours at a time, the mother who moves from zoo exhibit to zoo exhibit with her two children. Deeply connected to her children and the animals, the mother teaches and laughs and shows her love to everything as she moves through the park. In each example, the person is engaged in eudaimonic living.

A eudaimonic life is about the discovery of who you are. It's the opposite of striving. You are not forcing but you are being moved. When you get off the path of striving, of forcing desired outcomes, you can focus on your interior power, who you are, and what you are here to do in this life. You can live in the moment, addressing reality as it comes.

As you are reaching for the stars of your individual human excellence, you also need to grow down into your humanity, as deeply as you can, to stay rooted. A balance between the heights of potential and the weaknesses inside you, your darkness as well as your light is a part of the personality of a person living a eudaimonic life.

Eudaimonia is not living for a life of pleasure. The good life Aristotle referred to was not one of pleasure, but one of the filaments, the deep immersion into something meaningful, a life of enjoyment. Pleasure is different; it is the absence of pain. But pleasure has diminishing returns. In pleasure, nothing really happens inside of you. Enjoyment however has accelerating returns. Pain used skillfully creates remarkable humans.

Flow is a key aspect of eudaimonia; it is autotelic (a state worth pursuing for itself alone) and an important component of creativity and well-being. The more you practice being in autotelic experiences, the more you tend to want to be in them. You seek to replicate those types of experiences across the whole of your life. With each experience, your soul touches something, and it will want more.

Contributing to the whole is another key aspect of eudaimonia. Culturally, we deem those who follow their own path "selfish." But eudaimonia is liberation, and as such it is inherently unselfish. When you liberate yourself, you give people an example of freedom. With that freedom, you liberate others. By liberating yourself, you free people from your judgments, expectations, or ideas. And you cannot do this from a place of deprivation. You cannot approach the world with a "you owe me" attitude. The art of soulmaking calls for us to offer our gifts to the world so that we will make it and yourselves stronger and more alive.

This is total anathema to what the rational mind wants. How would we ever get our kudos in this system for being strong or thriving? How would we affirm and cure and heal? How would we connect with people, if not through this universal meeting in pain? What would the mind chew on or organize around? How would we employ our energies?

The life force might suggest that even the fact that the rational mind wants to hold onto the problem, it is not a problem; it is all an opportunity to play. This is simply energy that wants to express creatively. The rational mind has been so caught in the loop of bad-to-good that it has never caught a glimpse of an entire dimension of simple creativity, play, and exploration. Play is of the deepest order, what the rational mind dismisses precisely because play is such a high art. The rational mind, coarse in its hammer-and-nail mentality, has no idea where to begin and how to leave the side of the pool.

Play then is to initially liberate the mind. Life does not say, *Don't look*. It says quite the opposite: *Look with eyes that can actually see*. Life would dive right in and get stuck and lost. It would go deep into suffering. It would be brought down into the darkness to learn, step by step, how to dispel the delusions. It would put itself in the line of fire to know from within how to make it out with the playful mind intact, and with greater resilience and resourcefulness. Life may not change much, but how we see it changes entirely.

A man was in the midst of a terrible legal battle with his soon-to-be ex-wife, and access to his children was on the line.

His determination and ferocity were relentless. In between depositions, he left for a corporate baseball practice, leaving the lawyers speechless. *How could you go do* that *in the middle of* this? they wondered. He returned fresh, alive, and recommitted. He played, connecting with the energy and flow of the game, and was ready for reengagement with a difficult task. That play also created space in his mind where new possibilities could flow in; he would take the children for weekends and three uninterrupted months each summer. She agreed and the arrangement was done. He could see because he played.

Life flows when we admit our animal side, our endless daimonic cycling between the dark and the light, and admit that the animal naturally loves to hunt. It is either going to hunt down problems or else it is going to hunt down discoveries, creative ways of seeing things, and the processes of how things work. As a result, the senses will grow keener because in play and discovery, because we are interested, this sharpening naturally happens. Everything becomes of consequence. If we play hide-and-seek, we open our acuity, our sensing organ, in every direction.

If the organizing principle of the mind becomes the pursuit of a more artful and creative expression of life, then everything is of interest. The animal is put back into the wilds of the mind, back into its natural habitat, and not made to entertain itself with limited range, limited space, and always being watched in an artificial environment. When it is no longer pent up and is free to explore, the sense of discomfort resolves.

We take a simple and radical stance to life. Not, "How do we fix what is broken?" With that approach, the best we get is "unbroken." We ask, "What is possible and who do we need to become? How do we become that to discover?"

*"We are never more fully alive, more completely ourselves, or more deeply engrossed in anything than when we are playing."*

~CHARLES SCHAEFER

*"This is the real secret of life – to be completely engaged with what you are doing in the here and now. And instead of calling it work, realize it is play."*

~ALAN W. WATTS

## Integration Exercises

- Write down a "problem" in your life. How did you feel writing it down?

- Now draw or paint your problem, write a story or song about it, or rap it out.

- How do you feel now?

- In this way, you "play" instead of "solve" perceived problems, neutralizing their emotional hold on you. Do you see options you hadn't prior? The way forward can naturally reveal itself.

"I've been through a lot throughout my entire life, and growing up without a father was the hardest. A lot in my life has changed for the better, and I've lost a lot of family through these hard times of need, including my mother last year. Losing her while in prison was the most pain I have ever felt. My mother was my rock who kept me breathing, my support, and now everything has gone downhill. But while I've been doing this book, The Art of Soulmaking, I've gained a lot of new people in my life that do really care, and from the bottom of my big heart, I honor and adore the fact that someone (my pen pal), who is still living life, being your age, is a gift from God."

~James Dunn, Eastern Correctional Institution, North Carolina

# LOSING CONTROL SKILLFULLY

**Losing control upsets many; they feel ashamed or humiliated by it. Soulmakers see it differently. We believe that surrender is something we all long for, and in this lesson we work through how it's done constructively.**

I f we think we always want to be the one on top (the predator, the controller, the winner), we forget that we have a need to be warm and held inside the belly of the beast. We want to be possessed. That impersonal longing has zero rational discrimination and is built into all of us. It can present as addiction, yearning, obsession, something activated within us that calls to be taken. We hunger for a loss of control.

If you do not believe it, walk into a bar on any given night. Everyone is chasing a taste of being possessed by drink, laughter, dance, music, connection, the promise of sex. They long to be spirited away into oblivion where the bills aren't due, and everything appears available.

Go broader with the definition of "possession" and you have a painter or a writer or a biochemical researcher or teacher who, when engaged with their work, looks up at the clock and sees that six hours have passed in a second. The people are "possessed" by a calling that, once engaged, feels like flying.

Possession underlies our search for a mate; we may want to abandon ourselves to another human being or the whole of life. Society tells us this is good, becoming one mind, one heart, each possessed by the other.

Our culture takes a self-involved, controlling dominator view to all this. The fear of the psychedelic experience is quite literally the fear of losing control. Bars and liquor stores abound, all controlled by laws and regulations attempting to manage the outcome of consumed liquor. You can verify the effectiveness of this approach by looking at prison populations, broken marriages, car

*"For me the experience of writing is really an experience of losing control....I think it's very much like dreaming or like surfing. You go out there and wait for a wave, and when it comes it takes you somewhere and you don't know where it'll go."*
~MARGARET ATWOOD

crashes, and the emergency room on Saturday night. Dominator types don't understand that it's not important to maintain control if you are not in control in the first place.

The masculine world of achievement and laws has come down hard on the loss of control. The American government banned the Ghost Dances of the Native Americans and the Catholic Church forbade ecstatic dancing of pagan cultures hundreds of years ago. Even "raves," so popular a few years ago, were staged out of sight or often underground. In 1969, America was appalled by the sight of Woodstock with thousands of young people dancing in the mud; it was outrageous. The 1960s were all about the loss of control, and the ideas unleashed then have since swept the world several times over. The shamans use spirit drumming and Sufis twirl, chasing a feeling of euphoric improvisation; they move where impulse takes them. In this way, they become the music, they become the beat, leaving no space between themselves and the thing itself. The total connection and the human longing for it will never go away, no matter how far underground it is driven.

We veer toward acceptable versions of this: We cloak it in other language, but this acts only to distort love and drain the desire for possession of its potency. Without permission to let go, our lives grow heavy and overburdened with responsibility. The rational mind gets ever more demanding and keeps us in a chronic battle against this desire to allow ourselves to be taken over and possessed.

*"Care about what other people think and you will always be their prisoner."*

~LAO TZU

One of the great paradoxes of life is that in order to surrender, we need to take responsibility for everything inside of us: the nurturing mother, the steady provider, and the busy worker as well as the blamer, the taker, the pretender. Our life force points us toward the discarded parts of ourselves that signify what we too often see as weakness: the part of us that caves in, the doormat, the desperate one. If we allow the feelings of shame, inferiority, and self-betrayal around the loss of control to rise, it unleashes tremendous stuck energy and makes it available to us. We then begin working with that energy for possession by our creativity or calling.

Only then do we realize that nothing we do can make us wrong. Only then can we step into a seamless reality where we can love ourselves with the heart of compassion and allow the armoring to come off all our ideas, in response to what our deeper selves have been asking.

Your soul is calling you into surrender and possession by forces that you have never been and will never be able to control. But you can work with it and use it for a deeper, more satisfying life. The out-of-control will never stop coming at you; that energy is all part of the great Mystery, so start working *with* it.

When we work with energy, we develop the capacity to listen and respond to a deeper voice. We hear our inner voice. We discard the scripts based on ideas rather than felt truth, the truth that resonates in the body. Our sense of "good" and "bad" is dynamic and fluid. We lose control and return with renewed insight and vigor.

Life meets in Rumi's field beyond wrongdoing and rightdoing. Loss of control is not to be feared; it's to be *used*. Besides, what ever made you think you were in control of all this?

*"If you don't feel that you are possibly on the edge of humiliating yourself, of losing control of the whole thing, then probably what you are doing isn't very vital."*

~JOHN IRVING

*"Dear Fellow Human Being, You are born wild, You do not deserve to be tamed!"*

~JASZ GILL

## Integration Exercises

- Can you describe the last time you lost control?

- How did it feel just before, during, and after this event?

- What was scary?

- Did your fears become true? If they did, did the experience match what the fear told you it would be? How did it or didn't it?

- How would you know you have let go?

"I truly believe and embrace the statement 'You can live free inside of prison.' I'm living proof. I'm freer in here than I was on the outside, out there. I was chained down by addiction, gang lifestyle, abusive relationships. Yet, I was living in the 'free world.' However, these things kept me imprisoned. Here, behind these walls, I'm totally free, my spirit soars untethered."

~Jennifer Barela, Central California Women's Facility

# TURNING ON THE LIGHTS AND KEEPING THEM ON

## LESSON 19

This lesson brings together many skills—exploding tumescence, alchemy, working with the daimonic—to demonstrate a woman who can stand in her power anywhere. This is where you learn how to change a room by entering it.

Throughout the previous eighteen lessons, we've been digging and building, and we now enter the phase where we can see the entire house: from wiring and plumbing to landscape and interior design. Congratulations, we know it is not always easy.

You've likely learned the value of taking beliefs and emotions that do not serve you and exploding the energy by releasing shame, self-loathing, and denial. As you sink down into your body to be with the difficult emotions, from there, your body will tell you the truth, *your* truth, not some institution's or family member's or lover's truth. You can understand that your feelings are yours and can never be wrong; you wouldn't be here if you were not perfect.

By clearing out space inside your soul's home, you made room for new thoughts, sounds, and energies. By the time we make it to this stage of expression, the process is like a handmade glove: The fit of it is so impeccable and true to us that no matter what it looks like on the surface, it will have the transmission of congruence and truth to it. You meet reality with this new process. Here is where to take all of your newly acquired skills and put them into place, transforming pain, anger, and resentment into creativity and thus, life.

Oftentimes, what these lessons show is that the tricks our intellect so cleverly devises are of absolutely no use in the making of our soul. All the rules and regulations and laws and courtrooms could not sort out that chaos. And that's exactly as the soulmaker wants it. That's for us to use in the art that is our life. The descent can be overwhelming. It can feel like we have entered a din

*"As we advance in life it becomes more and more difficult, but in fighting the difficulties the inmost strength of the heart is developed."*

~VINCENT VAN GOGH

of chaos. The tumescent mind allowed for no disruptions of the static self because loss of control is shameful, unacceptable. Entry into the valley of the body is rich with sound and colors and sensations—mayhem. It takes time to sink into the seamless tapestry of it and to live in an open exchange with life. And when we do, we find a dynamic stillness and a sense of self that has real power.

Remember, anger is always tumescence, invariably taking us outside ourselves. Allowing anger to build up, or pretending it is not there, does not mean we are not tumesced. By ignoring it, we may hit a point where we need to express it, and it will come out unconsciously. Soulmaking wants us to trace the anger back inward to find its initial form, the sensation, without the story on top. Bringing it back into ourselves results in an internal locus of power. It is the first step toward our anger no longer being something that happens to us. If we focus on something outside of ourselves, it results in a loss of power. That's why we say, "Stay on it," because the answer will always arise from within.

We do not stop at feeling angry; we let ourselves feel it all the way through until the charge runs out. You may resist feeling certain feelings again, but be assured, once you go down, look at the sensations, and explode their grip on you, new life rushes in. We draw the energy that was trapped in resentment and anger back into ourselves, aiming it back in, so that we can harness the power of the impulse for directed purposes. That's how we rise in our power and take it into the world.

Eventually we want to even be able to transform resentment to the level of impulse. To do that, we must trace the resentment back through the stage where it was the emotion of anger in order to get back to its initial impulse. We must be willing to go there and sit with the anger, feeling through it without falling into it, in order to return to the level of impulse.

The most extreme form of resentment is punitiveness. We can only get that far outside of ourselves, out to the punitive self, when we forget that we are connected to everyone and everything. We must be disconnected to be in that place. Call it "compartmentalization" or whatever you please, but this place is

*"I sat with my anger long enough until she told me her real name was grief."*

~C.S. LEWIS

dangerous and not to be trusted. This is the place a soldier lives in so that they may kill. To trace our way back through all that self-will, we must trace back to the contemptuous self, to the outraged self, to the resentful self, to the angry self—and finally to the impulse of no-self. The self felt powerless and built up layer upon layer of negative emotion, but the self did not begin with all that baggage. The distance from the contemptuous self to the no-self is a stark measure of how far we have gotten away from ourselves by the time we became punitive.

Stay in yourself and with yourself and, wherever you go, you'll be in power. You will change the room just by entering it. We watch this magic again and again. You will begin attracting what you've become: calm, centered, and able to move through almost anything. Other powerful people will naturally be drawn to you; like responds to like. Others won't quite understand how you do it. The world spins, but you stay put in a quiet middle, living inside what instinctively feels good and right.

When no longer fighting your internal war, you begin working with life's energy, letting it flow into you and inform your every action. As you've come to understand yourself, you gain an understanding of and empathy for others. As you have come to accept the belief you yourself are perfect, you'll be able to accept that the world is also perfect. You are not here to impose your will on it, but rather work with it and transform its energy into creation, our reason to be.

As you rise in your power and step through your front door, others will respond to you in new ways. Their felt sense in their bodies will alert them to an approaching lion, a courageous, clear-eyed, completely confident animal free on the plains. In this way, you inspire all that you see. You change everything by simply changing your insides and staying with yourself, wherever you are.

*"Freedom is what we do with what is done to us."*

~JEAN-PAUL SARTRE

*"When there is no enemy within, the enemies outside cannot hurt you."*

~WINSTON CHURCHILL

## Integration Exercises

- Make a list of things you've never imagined you could do.

- Take a risk. You can afford it now. Do some of them.

- Write about how your body felt, your emotions, the sensations.

"*I love people. I don't always like them. I love the difficult people. When you give someone love and patience, regardless of their bad attitude, they feel it and it makes a difference.*"

~Kelly Sorrell, Central California
Women's Facility

# WITH INTERNAL WEALTH, GIVING BECOMES RECEIVING

## LESSON 20

**Acknowledge a request; the Universe has its hand out to you, asking something. Conversely, never hesitate to make an offering of your own. Learn the power of the offering and its ability to strengthen connections to each other and the world.**

I n the world *from below*, the place of soul and shadow, the origin of our life force, our angels come to us with hands outstretched, asking for help as often—if not more—than those who come with offerings, with gifts. We forget that love is experienced whether it is coming in or going out. We are built to respond to need in others. It wakes up something inside of us; every single one of us has it. Under the most hardened shell is this imperative.

Yet we have not necessarily had the framework to understand that life's energy, traveling equally from "heaven" above to the darkness below, and vice versa, can evolve this instinct for our benefit, can use this in service to our calling. When something or someone needs attention and love, and we give it, we are pulled out of our tumescent self-circulation, our egoism, and are drawn into the world where life is. We forget our problems and therefore ourselves, so engaged do we become with others.

What can feel to the tumescent mind like an inconvenience, a favor we are doing for someone else or a "contribution" we are making, is actually life with its annoying ways to yank us out of our tumescent fog. Life does not need to have the upper hand to be the bestower of good. It also does not mind being a little tricky. It is simply the open hand, offering or receiving, emptying or filling, depending on which is of greater benefit. Life gives the energy; it knows what you need. Don't argue with it. Just reach out your hand and see where it takes you.

This is where life may break into our guarded ego, using our own programming, with the opportunity to get out of the tape

*"Give, even if you only have a little."*
~BUDDHA

189

loop. This is challenging from the scarcity mindset that believes everyone wants something from it. In linear time, the tumescent mind is desperately trying to run from problem to solution, and will see any request for assistance from the world as a nuisance, a distraction from the hard work of earning goodness. We may be so hypnotized by the clock that we miss the request altogether, or race past it in utter blindness to the reality around us.

You've delved into your internal power, and this is another aspect of rising inside of it. You are not exhausted by living because now you have the tools to keep recycling what doesn't suit you into what does, such as flow, love, mastery, creation, and genius. You can meet whatever reality rises before you, because you know you can use it for wisdom, for creating, for art. You are not here to change reality—quite frankly, no one of us can. But you are here to "approve" of it, accept it, and respond, or not. Whatever happens, you *use* it to power you.

No you didn't want to drive to little league practice; it's not your week. In the car to the field, a young player expresses fears about his abilities. In a two-minute exchange, you offered support and love to that boy, and he went out and hit his first home run ever. As a soulmaker, you understand what you needed most in this world was to offer love and see where it went. Another scene might have you take over for a colleague who needs to make an emergency trip. Upon her return, she embraces you and says, "Thank you. I got to say goodbye to my father." The stakes change when you see how extending yourself and making the offering can change a life in such a way.

When life appears dressed as an outstretched hand asking for change, and we realize it when we offer it, we are the recipient of change in consciousness. This one moment shifts the sticky, inward-seeking mind that can only entertain itself by manufacturing and solving manufactured problems outward. Extending your hand opens a mental window, letting out all that is stuck and stale. You need this. When you offer love, it is for you *and* the other, but it is predominantly for you, with a vote of confidence in the Universe.

Abraham Lincoln, the guiding angel of the modern United States, presents a mesmerizing study in acknowledging the offering. Lincoln did not come to the office of president with the intention to abolish slavery; his contact with so many bloody Civil War battlefields did that slowly over time. Perhaps without even knowing it, he was transforming; and when the offering presented itself, he moved on it.

In the last phase of the Civil War, Lincoln made slavery illegal in the North and the border states between North and South for the simple reason that he needed more men to fight for the Union and win. It worked, and Lincoln was reelected. Still he resisted total emancipation of the slaves.

Then the offering happened. In between the election and his second inauguration, the President received a letter from an enslaved woman in a border state who asked a simple question: "Am I or am I not free?"

Imagine a slave, a woman no less, reaching toward the President of the United States, asking for something as precious as her freedom. Her hand, outstretched to him, created yet another epic shift in a man who had freed slaves from a pragmatic point of view. Their freedom had not begun as a moral decision, but it ended as one. In his second inauguration speech, President Lincoln said the Civil War dead presented a counterweight to 250 years of the blood of slavery, and he began feverish work to give former slaves the vote. He succeeded in passing that legislation in five weeks, and within days, he was murdered by an assassin's bullet.

Life presents itself as a need in another, and it will be strong enough to break through the armor of proving ourselves, and draw us into our own spontaneous, natural, and trembling-hearted response. The history and experience we are trying to run from or conceal becomes the very tool we need to help the other. It transforms and, in the moment, what was ugly in us becomes what gives us credibility, of understanding experientially what another person is going through. But this can only happen when the heart of need in one is connected with the heart of surplus in another. Lincoln developed that heart under great pressure. Could you?

*"The best way to destroy an enemy is to make him a friend."*

~ABRAHAM LINCOLN

*"Act of giving something to others is an art of flowering your heart."*

~VINAYAK

*"Where there is love, there is life."*

~MAHATMA GANDHI

Our story is rewritten before our eyes into something useful, every time we accept the offering, whether it is given or received. We get to empty out what was so uncomfortable inside of us that it gave us the sense there was a problem. In that connection, both giver and receiver are charged with life's power of give and take that occurs as abundance. If you have it, you give it. If you need it, you take it. In this way, we connect and care for each other. What looked like a waste of time in our busy day is translated by life into moments of profound connection and understanding. In the world of eternal time that is the Universe, there can be no such thing as a waste of time.

## Integration Exercises

- Write about something you did not want to do. What was it? Why did you resent it?

- Describe what you felt as you did it. Did anything about it surprise you? Did you smile? Laugh? Connect?

- Could you stay in this moment, doing something you didn't want to do, and open your heart to it?

- What did you learn?

*"My relationships with inmates and staff are way less strained. We have mutual respect for one another. And then my family has noticed a big change in my attitude and are so stoked by the sincerity that I have for this fundamental change in my life."*

~Elle Marteeny, Mendocino County Jail, California

# INTIMACY IS THE ANSWER

# LESSON 21

Intimacy and relationships are everything to the soul. Nothing can be disconnected from anything else; Earth works together. Explore how to strengthen your bonds and your love, melting preconditions, competition, and enmeshment.

Relationship is not *on the path* of Eros; relationship *is the path* of Eros. The mutual reciprocity between friends and our truest friends includes a largely unspoken agreement to make overt the inner workings of life. The mutual influencing that is always happening under the radar is the primary form of communication. That is the agreement on the Erotic path.

This agreement requires everything of us, because we are now responsible for what most people scarcely recognize even exists. We are responsible at the level of the unspoken, the un-heard, and the unexpressed. We are responsible for bringing our-selves to those depths, gaining fluency, and then operating with pitch-perfect response in accord with the laws.

This is where the soul you've been building begins to truly hum. This path, as mentioned, is about neither union nor sep-aration, but the dynamic life force that lies between everything, this force called intimacy. Exquisite care must be taken to ensure the well-being of this fragile force. To take exquisite care requires a relinquishing of all that is in between. Our life efforts must be dedicated to the hyper-focus required to maintain attention there, when either the force of another or our own selves threat-ens to pull our attention too far toward either one.

There are several obstacles to the hyper-focus that the path of Eros requires: withholding and withdrawal, avoidance and es-cape, and comparison.

## Withholding and Withdrawal

In the world of appearances, an action precedes (more often than not) what is regularly viewed as transgression. In the world of Eros, it is recognized that the root cause of gratuitous suffering is

*"Friendship is the hardest thing in the world to explain. It's not something you learn in school. But if you haven't learned the meaning of friendship, you really haven't learned anything."*

~MUHAMMAD ALI

*"Friendship is born at that moment when one person says to another, 'You too? I thought I was the only one.'"*

~C.S. LEWIS

*I can be honest about any relationship, and I can be available for any expression, positive or negative.*

disconnection. The greatest culprit of transgression, by the time it makes it to the world of appearances, is disconnection—which is most often rooted in withholding and withdrawal.

Think about painful events: the day he walked out of the door; the Friday afternoon when you were laid off; the morning you were stood up for brunch. Ask yourself, did those events take place with no indicators, no clues that a "transgression" was about to take place? Chances are, had you stayed present and in connected communication with the other, you would have felt this, talked about it, understood the dynamic. You weren't broadsided at all; you were disconnected.

We go against our very nature when we withhold and withdraw. We are born to know and share. Withholding love, truth, resources, attention, connection, and self violates natural law and necessarily erupts, at some point, on the surface as harm.

The only thing that activates shared inner seeing is wholly offering oneself. Once this is done, all see the same thing.

## Avoidance and Escape

Humans practice avoidance and escape from the workings of life. It could be that we escape through things that separate us, such as addiction, or things that separate us through union, such as spirituality. (Attend a small, closed religious group, break a rule, and face judgment. It's a tale as old as organized religion.) Avoiding the middle world where we all meet as humans is an obstacle to ever knowing unconditional liberation. This avoidance also permits us to live in a false identity of one who knows, when we do not know.

We are not speaking of a "period of mourning" or "taking a sabbatical." Avoidance and escape are about opting out of a state of connection with other human beings. In that state, you can no longer know who you are or rise in your power, because you are disconnected from everyone and everything else; you left the building and abdicated all. If you don't have connection, you've lost access to the life force. And because we identify with what

*"Something we were withholding made us weak, until we found it was ourselves."*

~ROBERT FROST

we are connected to: Mrs. So-and-So; John Smith, Esquire; John, father of Billy; or Sue Parker, MD. If we withdraw connection, our identity dies.

## Comparison

Comparison is fundamentally an aggressive act whereby we size up another in order to determine our relative position, and whether or not we can fulfill the edicts of the tumescent mind to win, be better than, or be right. Comparison is the consequence of not giving oneself over fully to the relationship.

Intimacy is a faculty that imposes no conditions other than the reception of another. It requires no commitment, no agreements, no special status, no kindness; only the choice to apply that faculty to connect with another person.

Sadly, what often passes for intimacy is enmeshment, a subtle form of hostage-taking. Think, *He can't leave me, I own half the business.* Or, *If she moves, I'll quit paying child support.* In this dynamic, we grow smaller rather than bigger, and less available for our lives. This kind of conditioning-driven relating, focusing primarily on this other person, is a subtle form of ego extension. This does not bring us closer to accessing the state of mind we seek, which is more akin to the breath than it is to any gripping or striving. It does the opposite of what true relating aims to do, which is to dissolve the sense of a separate self.

Enmeshment just gives our separate self the illusion that the other person will provide us safety or refuge from the world, by allowing us to stay away from it. But remember, if the ego is anything, it is isolation. Only now, we are in isolation with another body.

*"I will not reason and compare: my business is to create."*

~WILLIAM BLAKE

*"Only fear is restrictive. Love is expansive. And I wonder, since fear of enmeshment impels us to avoid commitment and fear of abandonment makes us possessive, what type of evolved relationship can emerge once those wounds are healed?"*

~NEIL STRAUSS

## True Love Is an Act of Becoming

Most people approach love as a sedative, when in fact it's a call to wake up, which is the only way that we'll ever be able to stop seeking external things to calm our nerves. What most people call love is in fact a good nap with company, a way to avoid our life without having to feel lonely, where two minds can agree to be only half aware together so that, in this state of merging, they can live half asleep as one and be safe. The way most people say, "I love you," is by saying I'll be half the person I was prior to you," as is often witnessed by the "coming back to life" people have after a breakup.

True love is a stealth act, one that in the world of mass production could seem too high-maintenance, too time-consuming, or requiring too much attention. Indeed, love demands a moment-by-moment, engaged attention. Yet the rewards are great. When we liberate something that has been caged, a pure line of devotion opens. More importantly, in the process of developing the attention we need to ensure our loved ones are genuinely loved, we become the person we have always wanted to be.

This is the secret gift of true love—it demands that we develop aspects of ourselves that are most needed to evolve us into who we are: beings capable of unconditional love.

If we are lucky, we instinctively know this unconditional love; we felt it from a parent or someone in our lives at some point. Evolving into a human being who can do that with everyone, not just their own children, is a thrilling state indeed. Loving unconditionally is the top of the mountain, the very state that holy men and women have chased for thousands of years. Through soulmaking, we learn what they learned. We can live in a state of intimacy with the world, both natural and human, by simply accepting it and loving what we find. You don't have to buy a car or play along with delusions. Just do you. Be present and emanate love. Nothing else is required.

*"The meeting of two personalities is like the contact of two chemical substances: if there is any reaction, both are transformed."*

~C.G. JUNG

*"As a kid, you learn to measure long before you understand the size or value of anything. Eventually, if you're lucky, you learn that you've been measuring all wrong."*

~FIRST LADY MICHELLE OBAMA

# Integration Exercises

- Have you ever asked too much of someone because you were frightened or felt alone or unloved?

- What happened with the relationship?

- How did it feel afterwards?

- How can you offer unconditional love to one person in your life?

- How did it feel afterwards?

*"Prison is the place where you cannot escape—not even from yourself. Lots of time for reflection. And as long as one takes the time to do such, like with this Soulmaking class, and meditation, then you can face yourself. And it is through that process of really 'facing' myself that I can see so much more light in the end. I can accept being here."*

~C. Gosztyla, Central California Women's Facility

# GIVING OURSELVES OVER

# LESSON 22

**You have all the knowledge now to live unconditionally. Explore what that means and how to do it, choosing life above all else. Feed off life's energies and pour it into creative work, a hallmark of genius.**

L iving what is true for you means you do not have to lead an off-the-rack life. Your house does not need to look like everyone else's. You are an individual. You are an adult, you can *choose*. A life driven by self-will, the "I must have a larger house; better business title" striving, might not be right for you. But there you are, chasing someone else's dream. Whose dream is it? Do you know? Is your life real for you? Or does it model what you saw in an advertisement for a bank?

Life doesn't care if we are ready for it or not. It comes anyway. What is required is a keen perception through all our senses rather than a capacity to shut down, to conform. Life requires awareness and attention. The rational mind is not of use; we must feel, see, and touch life's truth ourselves. If you meet life as it moves toward you, each moment, each point of contact, each charge of energy informs and shapes your soul so that it becomes deeper, more experienced, more complex. Moving with life gives us the resilience, power, and vision to show up for it.

Life has an unconventional way of guiding us. Life says the playing field is wide open; nothing is off-limits. It doesn't care if we are "virtuous" or not. It doesn't foist morality on us, and it does not impose limits. What it does is it asks us to feel it for ourself.

If we explore ourselves in truth, we quickly realize we all have the same drives. When we cut ourselves off from that truth, behaviors fall into judgments such as "good" or "bad." The drive is then fulfilled in secrecy, becoming pathology. It's not the drive that's harmful, it's the secret.

All our life force asks of us is that we operate for the benefit of all—the most benefit being access to pure, unadulterated life.

*"There are always flowers for those who want to see them."*

~HENRI MATISSE

*"There is a vitality, a life force, an energy, a quickening, that is translated through you into action, and because there is only one of you in all time, this expression is unique."*

~MARTHA GRAHAM

*"There is a force in the Universe, which, if we permit it, will flow through us and produce miraculous results."*

~MAHATMA GANDHI

*"Fruit and grain: a time of abundance.*
*Nobody dies, nobody goes hungry.*
*No sound except the roar of the wheat."*

~LOUISE GLÜCK, FROM
"ABUNDANCE"

A country in Central America is a perfect case study of operating for the benefit of all: Costa Rica. The country sold off its military and reinvested in its people, offering education and health care for all. Huge tracts of the country were put aside for conservation. The country's focus was on its natural world, attracting a multi-billion-dollar tourist trade. Costa Rica has no rush hours to speak of and, if you're hungry, fish or grab a chicken. It is life dedicated to life. They call it *pura vida* for "pure life." Costa Rica is in the top-five Blue Zones, where people live the longest and healthiest lives on the planet.

If we open our senses and connect to life's energy, we will be fed by this world, not exhausted by it. We will become so full we no longer need the gripping, the grasping, and consuming, all of which cause so much suffering. No longer driven by feelings of scarcity and lack, we begin to make choices that feed more life.

## Integration Exercises

- What part of your life is "cookie cutter," something you do (or did) because "everyone does it"?

- What would a custom life—one made especially for you—look like?

- Looking at your new life, how do you feel? What do you notice?

- What is one step you can take each week for the next few weeks to feel this life you see more fully in your body?

*"I am very optimistic about life and every day is the beginning of a new life, an opportunity to grow beyond the mistakes of yesterday. I am grateful for every day I am given."*

~Charles Finney, Union Correctional Institute, Florida

# HOUSEWARMING                    LESSON 23

T hrow open the front door and invite the world in; it's time to live in your new house of soul.

Mixing with guests after the previous lessons of exploration should prove interesting to a new soulmaker. Knowing who we are is a process of discovery that we make on the edges of identity—where we could have no idea how we would respond, no matter what we told ourselves until we were there. But beyond this, we cannot know who we are alone, because alone is not real. Who we are at every point is not a static self, but a process of mutually influencing reciprocity.

This is the point where a young child meets his or her first classroom, the alcoholic steps from the AA meeting room and operates in the world, or the inexperienced enters their first love affair. This is where we first learn the huge growth of connection. Everything and everyone we touch and that touches us shapes us; the touch is the thing.

In fact, we tap into the truth of who we are when we can connect with other nervous systems, extending consciousness into progressively further and further reaches. If the truth of this life is interconnection (and it is) there is simply no way to maintain the illusion that one can awaken without another one awakening. In other words, why build a house if you can't live in it? From this vantage point, the next master or world teacher will be the singular experience of a collective coming into connection. Just as Doctors Without Borders started with a few physicians with cowboy natures, a transformative collective formed, grew powerful, and fanned out over the world.

The teacher will be the connection itself, what lies between us; the place of promise will be the abundance we experience as well as the safety and love when connected into this whole.

**Enter the external world with your new skills and connect without judgment, rolling along with the energy of life. Engage and write about it. A subtle shift should be happening inside you. Fear has been replaced by an attentive curiosity; you can be with experience without hiding.**

---

*"May your walls know joy; may every room hold laughter and every window open to great possibility."*
~MARY ANNE RADMACHER

It will be here that we learn the mechanics and pronounce-ments of connection, that the whole exists as a form to protect the uniqueness of each. This is the unifying vision: Everyone must be who they are while being dedicated to honoring, supporting, and fostering their individual realization according to its distinct requirements. We must learn and keep learning what lights us up, creating more and more life in the moment. The more we do that, the more distinct the Universe's flow of energy becomes. As it takes hold of you, you move with it and others move with you. Soon the entire room is riding the same wave you're on.

In this way, we find ourselves together, awake, and at home. If we each endeavor toward this end, we discover that this process of interdependence and reliance organically draws forth the best in us and curbs the excesses—not to be good people, but because we have each placed our well-being in a collective pod. As such, we are responsible and are given the resources to realize who we are. Our thank-you for this is put back into the pot with care and attention, but also demonstrating the outcome of the investment in ourselves. We show the care we've taken with ourselves by turning it onto the world. In this virtuous cycle, growth begets growth. The cycle is also pragmatic in that it pushes us against things we would otherwise avoid. And for the care of the whole, we are required to release personal entitlement and preference in order to work toward the whole.

This is not done out of altruism but out of placing desire into a deeper, truer place. When we relate, tending first to what lies between us (whether it be love, tumescence, ambivalence, or anything in between) all three are taken care of necessarily. Because if we are not doing well as an individual, we are not do-ing well collectively. If the relationship is not doing well, neither person is doing well. Well-being becomes not something we do for someone else or do as a sacrifice. We cannot sacrifice our needs in the process either. All must grow and be tended to as necessary.

All of this is to ask, "If a tree falls in the forest and no one hears it, does it make a sound?"

*"Everything you do has an impact. Who you are—that you are—actually matters. In an interconnected world (the only kind we have), our actions and the actions of others are inextricably linked—we are always and forever in a dance of mutual influence with those with whom we directly and indirectly participate. It is the unavoidable reality of being social creatures, only magnified by an ever-increasingly complex and interwoven societal structure. We matter to each other."*

~PAUL GREINER

*"If I see it in nature, I know it will work in a home."*

~MILES REDD

We say no. If you explore yourself and find your genius, your mastery, your love, your truest self, and don't connect it to someone else, do you really have it?

We say no. Unless you share it and share yourself, how can we be sure you ever existed at all?

You've turned on your lights and now it's time to come in and feel the life, the energy.

That's it. After following the lessons thus far, your first housewarming is over. Your house is built, and everyone has been invited in. What you do from here is up to you. We hope a daily practice will stay with you for the remainder of your life. We hope that as you reveal more and more of your house of soul to others, they will also want to live in the same way, meeting life on life's terms. In that way, your unconditional freedom will inspire and free others. Freedom is viral; once you set it loose, it infects without prejudice. Once you free who you really are (your truth, under all the built-up confusions and past lies) others are freed to be who they truly are around you. Once you accept and love yourself, you can love and accept others more easily. Focus on what turns you on, and what turns you off grows smaller and falls away. In your turn-ons lie the answer to your mastery, your genius, your creativity, the reason you are alive.

Living inside your house of soul is living within your power. No one can do anything to you as long as you are there. You can be thrown in jail or tossed in a ditch, your partner may leave you, or your health may waver, but you know what you are built from: You built it yourself.

The last month of lessons are the walk on the tightrope. These are high-level soulmaking techniques, and it's now time to try them. With practice, they grow simpler each time. Soon you'll make these soulmaking moves almost unconsciously, just as the experienced pilot compensates smoothly in a downdraft.

*"The free soul is rare but you know it when you see it – basically because you feel good, very good when you are near or with them."*

~CHARLES BUKOWSKI

## Integration Exercises

■ At your party, which room did you like best?

■ In what new ways are you interacting with guests?

■ Which room do you need to spend more time developing?

---

*"After some time, you learn the subtle difference between holding a hand and chaining a soul . . ."*

~JORGE LUIS BORGES, FROM "YOU LEARN"

"I like the idea of seeking undesirable elements and finding ways to match them with other elements to create something beautiful and coveted. I am in an undesirable place that is not of my choosing and I struggle with all the emotions—fear and uncertainty being high on the list—of going through the motions and simply trying to carry on. I am not used to prioritizing myself and accepting help from others, so that continues to be an adjustment. The incorporation of reflection through the daily meditation, while challenging at times due to not wanting to feel vulnerable, does seem to be lessening the fear and anxiety associated with memories and thoughts that I usually bury."

~Hayley Gilligan, Central California Women's Facility

# LEAVING YOUR DOOR OPEN    LESSON 24

A challenging lesson, explore staying open while maintaining boundaries, a skill of great grace to anyone who masters it. Learn how to keep your gates open to kindness while maintaining a rail against harm.

*"No is a complete sentence."*
~ANNE LAMOTT

Remaining open while setting clear boundaries can feel like a Flying Wallenda walking a tightrope between the World Trade Towers. It can be scary as hell. At first, we may fear the tumescent explosions and the "they won't like me anymore" feel of it all. But like a Wallenda, the more you do it, the less you'll shake up there in the sky. You can be an open, receiving human being, completely at one with life's energies, without letting every bug drag you off your sweet spot.

Remember our friend who used to go on vacation and lock herself in the room and cry for the first two days? The big-shot career woman who was so exhausted she wasn't quite human anymore? On one such vacation, she was standing on a beach in Hawaii and took a call from the office. A colleague was complaining about another colleague while making a pitch for a larger, sun-filled office. The colleague filled her ear with words like "project management" and "optimal productivity." She went into "robot" mode, her usual fallback position when barraged by work-speak, just as twenty tons of wild humpback whale breached 200 feet offshore. Talk about the force of life!

Our friend hung up the phone without thinking; she'd been pulled right into the magnificent energy of the Universe that is the reason we're here. The message was not lost, and our tumesced friend left the big career and rejoined life.

Soulmakers owe *nothing* to the nagging and annoying, the tumescent mind that suggests the soulmaker *owes* them based on their feelings of scarcity and lack. The only action the soulmaker is required to take is a nonaction. Just leave the door open. It is up to the tumescent mind knocking on your door to approach you with kindness. We are all adults, and the currency is kindness.

*"Whatever customs humanity had
Becomes waves of compassion.
Nothing with shape and dimensions
can keep still when passions move.
Start your lives over.
Everyone is totally forgiven, no
matter what."*

~RUMI FROM "THE WANDERING
ELEPHANT"

*"Reconciliation is more beautiful
than victory."*

~VIOLETA CHAMORRO

Nothing else will do. If the other can meet kindness with kindness, a reciprocity can open, and the soulmaker can give.

If the soulmaker gives into the relentlessness of a tumescent mind, the soulmaker just pours resources onto arid land. The entire exchange then becomes a situation of the soulmaker feeling good about himself by providing the "gift," while the recipient feels a backlash of shame and "owing" by getting more than she can receive. The tumescent mind loves playing the impoverished soul, the sacrificial lamb, the martyr. Feeding that type of mind is the road to nowhere. Our mission is not that.

Our mission is to stay in our power, living in a smooth tango with life's energies, making every connection and endeavor stronger and more useful as you go. That's how we change the world, not by giving into someone's demands for attention. That would make you sick in the long run. The suggestion is to turn back to your life force and move with it, letting the tumescent mind of the other go and do what it will.

Your tumescent friend can come back to you, but there is a condition: Your gate is only open to kindness. If the other returns with kindness and a genuine desire to meet life on life's terms, let her in. If demand starts back up, shoo her out of your yard.

Always be conscious as to how you expend your energy. Status, sex, romance, and money are not the currency. Stop spending yourself on what does not matter. Stand firm in your power and lean toward your life, not someone else's. *Yours.*

## Integration Exercises

- Can you identify a demanding person in your life?

- How do you participate with their demands?

- Does your method work?

- What relationships feel generative?

- What relationships feel depletive?

*"Soulmaking is a place for me to explore and look inside myself. I can work on my stored emotions. It's a place to have meaningful conversations where I am not afraid of letting people know who I truly am. It has given me confidence, compassion, and acceptance. I don't feel different or alone anymore."*

~Jennifer Vazquez, Central California
Women's Facility

# ADDITIONS, RESTORATIONS, AND DESIGNING NEW ROOMS

*Becoming* **is this lesson topic. Soulmakers have a resilience born of engaging with life, with trying, and with experiencing things for ourselves. Stretch your soul; that's how it stays flexible and alive.**

Soulmakers approach life and calling in one of two ways. The first is: We only say yes to something we want to say yes to. The second is: We say yes beyond our ability. In this second scenario, the "yes" without the knowledge we will succeed offers the greatest room for growth. The latter is where we find our resourceful mind, where we can draw even more creativity out as we meet every request with enthusiasm. Since we've never done it before, we're thinking on our feet, discovering for ourselves, in direct contact with life. When we say yes beyond what we know we can do, we get to create a game where there is no room for personality, no way out, and we either rise to the occasion, or we do not. What happens is *growth*.

The game we create is not for achieving a specific result, and it is not to "produce." It is for who we become in the process. That's why we say yes to follow a new thread and learn where it goes. To follow a new thread, you see more of yourself under varying amounts of pressure. To follow a new thread reveals more about life and it reveals more about you. We cannot become the person we want to become—a person of courage, confidence, and belief—unless we meet the level of intensity the world requests with a matching level of reception.

A young actor heard the words of the Founding Fathers forged into a magical rap. His initial reaction was electric. He wanted to

*"Every strike brings me closer to the next homerun."*

~BABE RUTH

*"When someone tells me 'no,' it doesn't mean I can't do it, it simply means I can't do it with them"*

~KAREN E. QUINONES MILLER

be a part of that rythmn on stage and went on to become Aaron Burr in the Broadway megahit Hamilton. When asked the secret to his success, Leslie Odom, Jr., said, "Trying."

He did not know he would land the role, but he was so drawn to it, and he had to try. That's you, saying yes before you know you can do it. That's you, growing because you try.

From the absolute yes to the doubt, we then move on to the next stage—the room of resourcefulness. Hopefully by the time we make it into this room, we are having fun. Here we get resourceful until the creative endeavor turns on. This is the stage with the highest growth (the most fun and the most challenging) because our doubt will match the resourcefulness. Our resourceful self is precisely what we are growing in this stage. We reinforce the "yes" mind, knowing we have successfully met these challenges before and look at new angles we can take. We never allow a single moment of "this cannot be done" to enter.

We are following the mindset that first, we believe we can do it, and then the skill follows. This is different from the conditioned mindset many come from where we make sure we have all the appropriate skills before moving forward. We set a low bar that guarantees success and keeps us in mediocrity instead of having us hit flow. We do not face challenges; we only apply ourselves toward that which we are exactly qualified to do. This is not that. This is applying ourselves toward what we feel we cannot do. Then once having landed the job, although everything can tell us we will fail, we know that is not an option. It is our blueprint to complete this, we would be betraying ourselves if we did not. We use the shame of previous failures, the desire to not feel that failure again, as an incentive not to fail. We have a no-option policy with ourselves here, such that if everything around us were to change, if everyone in our endeavor with us were to disappear, we would still be here. We take 100 percent responsibility for the success of this thing.

That's who soulmakers are.

Sometimes we will miss an opportunity. Our programs will say no when our soul wants to say yes. From there we can look at

*"If somebody offers you an amazing opportunity but you are not sure you can do it, say yes, then learn how to do it later!"*

~RICHARD BRANSON

the reasons we missed the opportunity. We can reverse-engineer what happened. What were our rationalizations and justifications to not go to the next level? Where did we choose comfort and familiarity over growing our soul?

If we are asked, we are always ready. Know what things you need to develop to be ready the next time the opportunity presents. Your life is there to support your soul and not vice versa.

Step into it and say yes. That's how you grow.

## Integration Exercises

- Can you remember a time when you said "no" because you were afraid or self-conscious and missed an opportunity?

- How did you feel?

- Are you ready to say yes without knowing you'll succeed?

"*I have a new understanding of listening to my body. It's amazing really. I have always written to myself and in this Soul Inventory, I've learned a lot about how beneficial this is, and now even more so because I know more about it and am able to be more in tune with myself. Meditation has helped me relax. Until doing this course I can't say I ever felt really relaxed at all.*"

~Tami Jade, Central California Women's Facility

# CLEAN YOUR HOUSE AS YOU GO

# LESSON 26

**Housecleaning: even your house of soul needs it. Do it as you move through your life, week by week. Build a rhythm to your practice where you carve out a little more time to go a little deeper into challenging feelings. Explode them regularly and turn them into creative power.**

Housekeeping is an important part of life, especially for a soulmaker. This housekeeping works with the energy you encounter as you go: life's energy. Instead of taking a day to clean the entire house, you wipe the shower every time you step out of it, leaving it primed for your next bathing session. In that way, you stay lean, ready for what comes rather than fretting about a bathroom you need to clean. You can move and you can flow with the demands and delights of life.

Keep soulmaking practices close to your heart; they will serve you well. Stay conscious of tumescence; it's all around you. When you walk into it, what are you going to do? Can you remain in power here and fire love back? As above, so below. The cycling between higher ideals and the soulful energy of life in the fertile dirt is constantly at work inside of you. Have you learned to feel these two states shift inside yourself, using this skill to create both light visions as well as dark ones? Can you blend the "seen" world into the darkness and make something new?

Use alchemy on the negative events of your life and transform them into creativity and gratitude. The job you lost was paving the way for the great job you have now. Your husband left you so that you could arrive at this new joyous place. All of it happens to help you be who you are destined to be. Use alchemy on it all, and transform it to gold. Learn about what turns you on, and do it, living in passion and genius for ever-increasing lengths of time.

And every morning, if you can, sit with yourself and listen to the vast silence inside your interior cathedral, your house of soul. Messages will rise from your body and mind. Listen to them.

*"I felt clean, all the bone-beaked loneliness birds banished, their rocky nests turned to river stones. Cool, clear water bubbled over them, streams in the desert."*
~BRYCE COURTENAY

*"His father had a dream to keep his hands forever clean. Joey wasn't clear if his father had ever understood that it takes a lot of digging in the dirt to do that."*
~WILLIAM GASS

That's the Universe speaking to and through you; it is a part of the Mystery and an infallible guide in living your life. Trust it and move with it toward what is true for you. You know, somewhere deep inside you, you *know*. Turn down the volume of the outside world and listen.

Soulmaking is about staying clean and staying lean. This diminishes suffering and the endless load of bad emotions. The time you spend "getting over it" collapses, and you come to understand at ever-increasing speeds. You learn acceptance of yourself and others. You learn to play with life, testing yourself and your abilities to ever-greater satisfactions. You create.

It's a simple process, though we had to pull it apart and take it slow to explain it. Now do it faster until it becomes second nature, and you can move through any stress or pressure with a smile and a toss of the head. You can do this simple, four-step process for masterful, high-level soulmaking anywhere, anytime, in the space your body takes up:

1. Experience the event.
2. Drop down into your body and feel it. Cry, shout, shake, whatever. Feel it and understand all the parts that bite and hurt. Try to trace the feeling back to other events like it. In this way, we break apart learned patterns of negativity and abuse.
3. Let your power, who you are and what you want to do, flow back into your body. What does the event tell you about what you will do and what you will not do?
4. Take it into the world with the knowledge that whatever you do, it will be the right, truest thing to do for you.

*"Listening is a magnetic and strange thing, a creative force. The friends who listen to us are the ones we move toward. When we are listened to, it creates us, makes us unfold and expand."*

~KARL A MENNINGER

## Integration Exercises

- During this lesson, take any negative event and use the four steps to cycle through it as quickly as possible.

- When you sank down into your body in Step 2, how did it feel?

- What were your conclusions in Step 3 and how did you carry that power into the world?

*"Freedom is a state of mind, it requires a certain consent to be in prison. Choices, desires and actions decide our level of freedom and incarceration, regardless of physical location."*

~Laura Lutrell Purviance, Central California Women's Facility

# LIBERATION

Liberation feels like riding the subway; you adjust as the car changes angles and rattles along the rails. It becomes intuitive and automatic. You meet the subway car on its own terms. That's what soulmakers do with life. We do not reject the "profane" for "sacred." We move between because our souls are strong; we are liberated. We are unconditionally free from external circumstances. We remain who we are despite any stressors. We don't long to escape to the mountaintop, we want to experience life and let those experiences run through our felt senses, our intuition, and our bodies. We want to feel it all. We allow ourselves to be changed by this form of surrendering, this liberation to what *is*. This takes and transmutes the experience of life into wisdom and intimacy. We can do all kinds of practices in between, but if we connect, move and love, accept and approve, we are engaged in the most advanced practices in life.

In liberation comes an adulthood of soul. Just as we raise a child, pouring love and care into it to set it free into the world, we care for our soul then let it go into the world to work with whatever it finds. Power occurs as resilience, a fortitude where we can be with life rather than seeking refuge in spirituality, retiring to the literal monastery, or attempting to enforce our spiritual dogma on it. We do not retreat inside ourselves; we always move toward life.

Liberation means there is no need to angle or steer our experience in any direction. We have less dodge and weave with phenomena, an "If I do that, maybe this will happen" approach to life. We stop foolish machinations and meet it all eye to eye, without hedging, withdrawing, or pushing past. In this way, we banish the exhaustion of "managing" life and feed off the endless energy of being in it.

**Reaching the top of the mountain, transcendence, that longed-for state where the interplay of creativity, power, connection, love, and turning on permeates everything. That's freedom regardless of circumstance. Transcendence equals unconditional freedom.**

---

*"Self-realization is liberation. Liberation is self-realization."*
~FREDERICK LENZ

We also discover that, as an extension of this, our relationships change. Our openness to the truth grows as well as our sensitivity to it. Others feel more comfortable communicating the truth to us without feeling that they need to do so with heavy pressure or evasion. Much of human communication is protecting each other's right to remain asleep. We collude in agreement to not speak the truth of what "might be in there."

A truth about the truth may reveal itself. We may have felt that there was some secret to life or that people have kept secrets from us, or that there has been betrayal as the result of secrets. But we discover that we can create an environment in ourselves, in our lives, in our worlds. Because we are not blocking truth, and are agreeing to receive it, our lives and the people in them feel free to reveal secrets to us about the nature of life, about who we are and how we operate, and what others connected to us see and feel.

Our question becomes, how open have we made ourselves to receive all this new information? How do we respond when we see difficult truths about ourselves? Do we quickly try to fix and conceal, or do we sit with it and ask the next question? Do we judge it immediately or do we get to know why it is there? When we feel that heavy pressure of the truth nailing us, do we squirm? Do we check out? Do we flail against? Or do we receive it? Can we even thank it for arriving? Can we feel that place where this truth upends any ideas of security? Can we welcome it as a friend? Or do we distract ourselves? Do we try to create a counter behavior? Do we threaten the world that if it tells us the truth in some way, we will harm it, harm ourselves, withdraw?

Liberation pulls us out of ourself and into the world where the laws of time and space do not apply. Liberation is truth, an ongoing, endlessly surprising adventure of a lifetime. It is living in a moment of wonder where there is no skin between you and the world. It is a rising above what is known, a direct engagement with the Mystery that is at the center of all our lives.

What more is there to learn?

That's just it; it never stops, any more than a tree stops growing. Your soul goes on forever, stretching out beyond our limited understanding and into all of nature, the cosmos and beyond. As Shakespeare said and science proved, we are made of star stuff. Stars are made of the same materials as found in our bones. We are both earth and sky, as celestial as swirling light particles and as firmly rooted in soil as a twisting bean plant. Our dynamism and growth can never be stopped. We are a part of everything, and everything is a part of us. We each embody life itself.

Finished? Hardly. Take a little rest and think about what you've learned. Then turn back to Lesson One and, like the early birds, rise and start again.

# EPILOGUE

Diving into the Wreck
I came to explore the wreck.
The words are purposes.
The words are maps.
I came to see the damage that was done
and the treasures that prevail.
~Adrienne Rich

During this journey of soulmaking, we've been guided to reunite the pieces into one. We've gone into the basement where the monsters are and flipped on the lights. With the false now removed, we have seen that we are each inherently magical, gifted, and visionary. We have been charged with a calling that, now accepted, has drawn us so far out beyond who we know ourselves to be, at such an accelerated pace, that we scarcely recognize ourselves after a short period of being "possessed" by our calling.

Building a soul is the work of a lifetime, the work that never stops—the work we are all here to do, and the work that must be done, because without a fully functioning soul—in you, in me, in everyone—we fail to learn, grow, and thrive. We do not meet our potential. The soul knows what it needs to move and grow, and with *The Art of Soulmaking*, we learn how to access our soul.

In this life, the call to each of us is the same: to grow strong enough inside ourselves so that we can connect and create art, relationships, a career, a life. This strength is what the soul craves. It's the call to know ourselves and stand strong in the whirlwinds, calmly building and reaching and connecting with others while staying firmly rooted in our individuality, what we each love to do, our desires, our essence, our soul.

The word "soul" has endless definitions, usually including the "immaterial essence" of a human being. That vague description doesn't get us far, so let's put a point on it. The soul is always cycling between light and darkness; the soul craves getting down and dirty as much as it loves the peace inside the light. The soul loves a bad girl just as well as it loves a good guy. The soul is evidenced by the messages your body sends, the twinges and tingles, as well as that bright explosion of paint you threw on a canvas that seemingly came out of nowhere. The soul is the voice in your head that says, *Do it!* And then, *Do it again*, driving you toward your particular genius.

We can hear the soul in the wild, high note rising above the band, and in the hunched-over form of the architect drafting at her desk. The soul moves fast and slow and every speed in between. It moves around inside of us, endlessly, then out of us and toward all that it feels, hears, smells, intuits, and sees. The soul is that sense of knowing when something is right; the soul, whether we are in tune with it or out of tune with it, guides our life.

Only you can tune in to your soul; it is unique to you. The soul has no rules. Like the tiger, the soul cannot be taken and domesticated. Even as we work on it and with it, the soul will surprise us. Even the greatest masters of the soul will trip and fall from time to time. But part of being a master of the soul is getting back up and moving on, because that is what life requires.

Know this: You have a birthright. You were born perfect, otherwise you wouldn't be here. Whatever has happened in your life, whatever you've been told or believe, you deserve to be a whole human; you deserve a complete life. You must understand this is the practice of a lifetime.

We pour countless hours into our bodies, our kids, our houses, our wardrobes, our jobs, even our companion animals, yet we devote no time to the most profound part of ourselves: our souls. We're not talking about learning the rules of religion; we're talking about the movement of the deepest, most complex part of your being that is specific to you. The methods to reach this essence are simple and work across the entire spectrum of humans. What rises, however, is not simple.

As we work to understand ourselves and our points of contact with the Universe—with the vital energy of life—we see each person's unique genius moving into view. As you strip away the harsh words and disappointments you may have experienced, you create space inside yourself that is empty, a void. That "new" space is where you are invited to live now, learning to convert any darkness into something of use in your life, something of beauty, not something that stops you. In this way, you will work with life's energies, rather than exhausting yourself in opposition and denial.

When you give yourself an opportunity to grow your soul, the transformation will take you far beyond what you thought possible in your life. The love and acceptance you develop for yourself will slowly bleed out into the world, creating connection. As you open yourself up to sit quietly and listen, you can hear what the Universe has been trying to tell you. This voice is never wrong. This is the sound of your soul, and we want you to learn to trust it. It's all there inside you—everything you need to live this life with elegance, true beauty, and deep satisfaction is there. That's where the voice that is your soul leads you.

# SOULMAKER'S MANIFESTO

We work with genius, the daimonic, the wildness inside us, the wolf. We carry hospitality, a handling of one another's worlds; we are leaders.

We move with an immediacy, a directness, an honesty that goes beyond mere truth.

We feel a loyalty, a "ride-or-die" attitude, that "there is nothing to lose," so reveal ourself, with no need to posture or conceal. We don't aim to be for those who hide their true selves.

We carry a self-possession that will not sell out or be made to conform. We carry little self-doubt and do not understand it in others.

We are hard core and carry a radical responsibility for our experience.

We refuse to take another's word for it; we are provocateurs and push boundaries in order to know for ourselves.

We exalt sexuality and passion and use our own bodies as laboratories to explore all states of altered consciousness, from meditation to obsession; we must know for ourselves how something works.

We are ruled by love but know the distinction between compassion and enabling.

We have cunning, using our eyes and ears to sense everything, seen and unseen, and move with a constantly awake, running assessment of our environment.

We love radical humor, and we love to play.

We may get our feelings hurt easily but exhibit extraordinary resilience.

We may seem insecure because we are sensitive, but we are indestructible.

We value effectiveness more than goodness.

We have true aim, both constructive and destructive.

We are solid all the way through, unbribable, because we do not value what many others in the world value.

We value our freedom in thought and expression.

We may seem impulsive, but we respond to what others do not see, sometimes five chess moves ahead.

We may appear volatile because we operate by a different code. If you understand that code, we are extremely predictable.

We have a tried, true, tested, and constantly refined method to our madness.

We are paradoxically dominant and submissive, introverted and extroverted.

We are often deeply alone, because we are different; our sensitivity is sometimes mistaken for trauma.

We respect genius deeply, but not authority without talent.

We can be repulsed by a lack of courage.

We can appear as shapeshifters to make it through the world, but we are deeply congruent.

We can seem contrarian to those defined by a single dominant culture, because we do not have a "party line"; our lives are custom.

We might appear idealistic but are truly rooted in realism and what it takes to create radical (as in rooted) change.

We are particularly appreciative of kindness and relate to animals.

We are associative rather than linear thinkers and see patterns and structures rather than mere content.

We are non-dual and move in light *and* shadow; we have no desire to only ascend or withdraw.

We are more often intuitive versus rational—although we can also be rational.

We experience flashes of genius which might be considered by some as narcissistic or grandiose, because it takes much to manage one's art, genius, or any extremes that mediocrity does not know.

We are often frustrated when others do not see or understand us, especially when we are judged by conventional standards that feel outdated or ignorant.

We are often labeled as arrogant when we are most often simply correct.

We are deeply committed.

We are hyper-focused with a full range of emotional expression.

We have an uncanny charisma and magnetism.

We hear one note and hear the entire song.

We are visionary, and we do not hold back, because to interrupt flow is death.

# SOULMAKER'S PROMISE

This journey is for all of us.

The work here presents in our lives everywhere; we are prepared for change.

Let soul become a passion, a pursuit; its growth and shape are as varied as individuals. Just as you chase a piano sonata or a four-minute mile, seek soul.

Practice, that daily reattaching to the eternal stillness inside, may seem difficult at first. Remember, it is better to push forward than to fall back into a metaphorical prison cell.

Through practice comes freedom, it's the process that outlines our true form and slowly carves away the rock created by layers of hurt and harm. Once you know yourself, no matter your circumstances, you are unconditionally free.

Listen to the body; intuition is precious and must be restored.

Write without self-consciousness; the page is the medium to work through hurt, disappointment, responsibility, and rage. Writing is a great way to bleed out the harm so that you may fill up with the good stuff.

Uncover your "turn-ons" and spend days there, creating. The more you live inside what you love to do, the more joy you generate.

As you uncover your own perfection, you feel it in everyone and everything around you; this leads to connection and intimacy, the food we all need and crave.

As you turn on, turn on other people. In that way, soulmakers heal the world by passing on the knowledge and setting the next person free.

# THE ART OF SOULMAKING
# PRISON LETTER
# WRITING PROGRAM

*he Art of Soulmaking: Prison Edition*, is an adoption of this book, made specifically for those in prison. This book is offered free of charge to the incarcerated across the United States, both as a physical book and on digital tablet providers.

As of Spring 2023, only two years since launching the book, over 20,000 people in prison have gone through the program. One aspect of this supportive, community-focused The Art of Soulmaking experience is the prison letter writing program. Through The Art of Soulmaking, people can sign up to have a pen pal with someone outside of prison who is also studying in the program. Pen pals can exchange letters using the integration questions for each lesson as discussion material.

Pen pals are paired by the Unconditional Freedom Project, a nonprofit organization. Through the organization's letter-writing platform, volunteers outside of prison can exchange letters with incarcerated pen pals anonymously and digitally from either phone, tablet, or computer. Hand-writing, envelopes, and stamps are not necessary. Volunteers' full name, email address, and physical address are never revealed to their pen pal in prison. Instead, all mail from both volunteers and the incarcerated are routed through Unconditional Freedom Project's PO Box and prison-tablet provider email aliases.

Pen pals are also offered support via volunteer mentors, available on text chat or phone call, who can answer questions and help review letters when writers get stuck. Each week, virtual community meetings are held in which volunteers have the option to attend and meet other pen pals, share experiences, and get questions answered.

Volunteering and training are free.

To learn more about volunteering or to sign up, complete the ten-minute certification and get started by visiting unconditionalfreedom.org/penpal.

# ADDITIONAL LETTERS TO THE NEWCOMER

To those considering The Art of Soulmaking:

Last year, I unexpectedly received The Art of Soulmaking in the mail. I read the introduction and was hooked. I got right to work that evening. Since that night, the program has greatly improved my life in prison and has provided me with tools that will continue to benefit me long after my release.

One of the first benefits I noticed was the structure and purpose the daily practices added to my mornings, when prison life feels especially slow and listless for me. Instead, I wake up, get a glass of water, work through my daily practices, and go about my day.

Each practice has become a fulfilling part of my days. My days feel incomplete without them now. The yoga is refreshing and relaxing. The meditation declutters the mind and helps me work through problems. The Soul Letters are cathartic, therapeutic, and insightful. I've found I now fixate on the negative less and my days pass more quickly.

Perhaps the most rewarding part of the workbook has been how it's encouraged and helped me to reimagine and reflect on how I can transform my time and suffering into something greater and beneficial to me and those around me. I've learned that my environment doesn't dictate my life or define who I am in this world. The program has helped me to actively practice contemplation and self-examination.

When I first began The Art of Soulmaking program, I encountered puzzled looks and questions as I did my daily practices. At first, I was a little self-conscious but this quickly passed. People got used to *my routine and some even grew interested in completing the program themselves.*

*Many of us in prison are seeking meaningful ways to improve our lives and form healthy routines, so sharing these ideas and tools has been another rewarding aspect of the experience. As you work through this program, I encourage you to share your experiences and workbook with your peers.*

*It's been said the hardest part of a journey is taking the first step. Now that* The Art of Soulmaking *is in your hands, I hope you'll do what I did and commit to following through with this course to its completion and giving its message and practices an honest try. I'm writing this nearly a year after beginning my journey and I'm incredibly thankful I happened across this program and gave it a shot.*

*It's my hope that anyone who may read this, chooses to utilize* The Art of Soulmaking, *and use their time to better themselves in ways that will persist far beyond the prison's walls and razor wire.*

*Best Wishes,*

*Thom*

Thomas is currently incarcerated in Virginia. He discovered The Art of Soulmaking while in prison at the age of twenty-nine.

*To* The Art of Soulmaking *newcomer, I began reading* The Art of Soulmaking *and participating in the AoS program as a result of my exploration in mindfulness. Over the past few years, my focus has been on mindful communication. I was exploring possibilities on how to manifest mindful communication into action (challenging my old thought and verbal patterns). I stumbled into this program. I read through the AoS workbook and was invigorated by the contents. The Soulmaker Principles in the workbook articulated concepts and ideas that had previously been only vague wisps of thought and intentions.*

*Participating in this program has solidified my opinion that true change comes through pausing and connecting with each other on a human-to-human level. Our emotions, our thoughts, and our actions are similar regardless of where we come from or where we find* ourselves in our present moment. When I think about what is needed to create human flourishing in our world, the answer always points back to connection, to fostering that understanding of shared humanity and interrelated welfare. To seeing beyond the labels put upon us, and opening the doors to the possibility of a new world that has space and understanding for all our lived experiences.

Learning how to see and live truth is a challenging pathway. The workbook offers tools to see situations with a little more clarity. Having letters with our penpals and meeting with other volunteers has been valuable in supporting my own efforts of internal reflection and transmutation. We come together to create community, support, and grace for the effort it takes to transform those aspects of ourselves that no longer serve us. It is helpful to converse with others who are also on the path of introspection and transformation of their pain into something greater than themselves. Participating in the Unconditional Freedom project has given me the opportunity to make connections with folks I might not otherwise have met. I have received a lot of wisdom I am able to put into practice in my own daily living.

There are many days I am distraught about the state of the world I find myself living in. The increased levels of violence against each other interpersonally, nationally, and globally are overwhelming. I see my participation with this group as an opportunity to put my values into action. I do this in an effort to serve humanity. To serve love, kindness, establish understanding with some who may have had a different life experience than I have had. In having conversations that enrich my mind and my soul, I am healed as much as I hope to offer healing. I am comforted as much as I hope to comfort. Knowing someone sees you, listens to you, and actually cares about you can have a deeply profound effect on a person's heart. If my heart can be softened and your heart can be softened, then the world is that much softer for everyone else.

Too often our society shuns those who are "others," and at a great loss. So often the perpetrators are victims themselves as a result of years of intergenerational violence and trauma. It is my opinion that the way to stop the cycle of violence and "othering" is to pause and connect with each other for conversations and to understand that when I hurt you, I am hurting myself. I hope by having these talks we'll develop more *understanding of ourselves and each other as fellow humans and work together to put more loving energy out into the universe. I want to love as many people as I possibly can in this world. I believe we are all one. I am hopeful that sharing my experience may motivate others to participate in this uplifting work.*

*Signed,*

*Mary*

Mary Stockwell-White has been studying The Art of Soulmaking for close to two years. She currently volunteers as a letter writer for Unconditional Freedom's Art of Soulmaking Prison penpal program, through which she exchanges letters with individuals who are incarcerated and are also studying the workbook.

# FROM THE AUTHORS

**Beth Wareham:** I am a longtime writer and editor with an extensive list of books behind me. I have written three of my own—two nonfiction and one novel—and have ghostwritten countless others. I pride myself on being a generalist, allowing for maximum learning as I go through life. I spent the majority of my career as a publisher at Simon and Schuster. An adventuress, I have tracked elephants on foot in Zimbabwe, kayaked with Right whales in the Bay of Fundy, and ridden across the Pampas of Chile. After I lost half of my family in a six-week period, my travels turned more inward. I stepped back from life for a year of what I can only call mourning, the first step in a long process of rebuilding my internal world after that trauma. I live in New York City with my husband and two cats, Carmelo and LaLa.

**Nicole Daedone:** I want to know life biblically, the way a man knows a woman, the way a lover knows a beloved. I want to know the water by getting wet. Theory, commandments, concepts leave me hollow. My driving questions when I come across dicta and dogma are, Is that true? Is it wholly true? Where and how is it true? For whom is it true and why? Can it withstand the test of time? Is it true for me as a woman? The last one has taken me off many a beaten path. Givens are often no longer givens when I ask this question. The world turns upside down. As a free woman, I want all things to be free, liberated from any ideas I would impose on them.

We are constructed of the divine. I believe everything—and I mean everything—when properly tended to, reveals an untold beauty. But my work is not as activist, reformer, saint, teacher, guru, or shaman—it is as artist. Erotic artist. The art I do is akin to found-object art: art made from what has been thrown away. It's an art that turns something back into itself. Like turning prisons into monasteries; the unconscious realm of sex into the spiritual plane of Eros; the degradation of addiction into the art of addiction that isolates the addiction drive for purposes of realization; the life sentence of trauma into human flourishing; the feminism of subjugated women into the feminine collective of inestimable power; those who have been canceled, exiled, and banished into the leaders of the next era; desertified soil into not only carbon-absorbing but nutrient-producing; hunger and food deserts into farm-to-table, free, pop-up restaurants; black culture into the black box for society that holds the secrets. These programs exist, and you can find them here: www.unconditionalfreedom.org.

I founded OneTaste to reawaken our connection with intimacy, with each other, and to the primal source of energy that drives our creativity—sexuality. I created a contemplative discipline around Orgasmic Meditation (OM) that offers an immediate experience of what happens when we unleash rather than repress who we are. Since then, we have gathered some of the greatest research psychologists and neuroscientists to study the intersection of sexuality and human potential, in the largest study of its kind since Masters and Johnson. We know that OM has perhaps the most powerful effect of any natural process on healing trauma, promoting well-being, and transcendental experience. I have gathered people and created systems so that the vision can be manifested and grounded in observable benefit.

My work remains as it always was: to turn poison into medicine and make it available to those who want it. But for those who need it, here is the conventional side of things: I graduated from San Francisco State University with a degree in semantics and gender communication. I cofounded the popular avant-garde art gallery, 111 Minna Gallery, in San Francisco's SoMa district before founding OneTaste.

I have appeared on *ABC News Nightline*, and my work has

been featured in *The New York Times*, *New York Post*, *San Francisco Chronicle*, and *7x7 Magazine*, among others. I've written for *Tricycle: The Buddhist Review* and I wrote the book *Slow Sex: The Art and Craft of the Female Orgasm* (Hachette, 2011). My 2011 TEDxSF talk on OM has been viewed over a million times on YouTube.com.

# ABOUT SOULMAKER PRESS

German philosopher Arthur Schopenhauer wrote that the truth comes in three stages: First, it is ridiculed. Second, it is violently opposed. And finally, it becomes self-evident. For those who can hear, truth in those early stages sounds like the whispering of the soul to itself. A relief, a resting place for the derided, the ostracized, the outsider.

Soulmaker Press is a full-service, privately held, international publisher, fostering avenues for writers and readers to explore new ideas in the space where intellect, science, the arts, and the mystical converge. We draw upon the writing and editorial talents of an international team to deliver the highest-quality reading experience, wherever books are sold.

Powered by Eros, in classical mythology the fundamental force in creation, our work is rooted in discovery and art, including works often considered taboo. We take special interest in the shadow, the unconscious, the creative process, and a feminine non-rational system of order. Precisely because it includes both the spirit and soul, the profound and the profane, emotions and the body, Eros offers a deeply needed perspective of unity that the world is sorely lacking. It's the magic that has been missing, and our books on spirituality, health and wellness, women, social reform, memoir, and science are intended to restore its intelligence to our lives.

Soulmaker Press is part of a greater initiative to reintegrate what's been cast out as unlovable. Initiatives include: breakthrough somatic modalities for healing trauma and expanding consciousness; rewilding land; creating programs for shifting prisons to monasteries that reintegrate the soul; prison gardens; and Free Food street restaurants in San Francisco and New York City.

Made in United States
North Haven, CT
08 November 2023

43716048R00143